All Hat & No Cattle

Lone Star Books®
An imprint of Gulf Publishing Company
Houston, Texas

All Hat & No Cattle

A Guide for New Texans and All the West of Us

Anne Dingus

Illustrations by David Maloney

All Hat & No Cattle

Lone Star Books®
An imprint of Gulf Publishing Company
Book Division
P.O. Box 2608 □ Houston, Texas 77252-2608

10 9 8 7 6 5 4 3 2 1

Library of Congress Cataloging-in-Publication Data

Dingus, Anne, 1953–
　　All hat and no cattle : a guide for new Texans and all the
west of us / Anne Dingus.
　　　　p.　　　cm.
　　ISBN 0-87719-351-7
　　1. Texas—Description and travel Miscellanea.　2. Texas—
Social life and customs Miscellanea.　I. Title.
F391.2.D54　1999
976.4—dc21　　　　　　　　　　　　　　　　　99-16451
　　　　　　　　　　　　　　　　　　　　　　　　CIP

Printed in the United States of America.

Printed on acid-free paper (∞).

Illustrations by David Maloney.
Book & cover design by Roxann L. Combs.

This book is dedicated with love

to my sisters and brother—

Jane Dingus Hildebrandt,

Nancy Dingus Crites,

and William F. Dingus.

Contents

Acknowledgments

No writer could finish a book without the help of many family members and friends. Isela Romero Redman, my children's wonderful paternal grandmother, and middle-school teacher Elena Bremer de Jarquín generously provided translations (and corrections!) for the chapter on Spanish; two other El Pasoans, John R. Karr and Marty Brown, lent handy advice and comments, too.

My chief musical consultants were the ever-helpful Jim Carroll and Kevin Dubose, longtime fans and students of Texas music. A superior resource is the collective brain power of my esteemed colleagues at *Texas Monthly*, particularly John Broders and Jane Dure.

Friends Stephanie Dodson, Cynthia Hudson, and Robert Zirl pitched in with encouragement and sympathy—as did my greatest fans: my father and mother and my sons, Philip and Parker Redman, who obligingly relinquished the computer on demand and cheered me with love, patience, and heart-warming remarks like, "Mom, you make the worst puns in the world."

I do? Thanks, guys!

Introduction

If you're a Texan, you *can* be in two places at once: the wild and woolly West of history and folklore and the urban, perturbin', high-speed, high-tech Texas of today. This book addresses that curious dichotomy, with an eye both to entertaining Texas natives who have long straddled both worlds and to educating newcomers who have proved their practicality and smarts by moving to our thoroughly modern millennial state. These essays cover a variety of subjects—animals, cities, food, fashion, Spanish, myths, humor, and entertainment—and each, I hope, provides ample amusement, as well as a few honest-to-God facts (and, if you're pun-allergic, perhaps a rash or two). I always welcome comments and grudgingly tolerate criticism; feel free to contact me at P.O. Box 1569, Austin, Texas 78767-1569. In the meantime, I hope you enjoy reading this book as much as I enjoyed writing it.

Anne Dingus
Austin, Texas

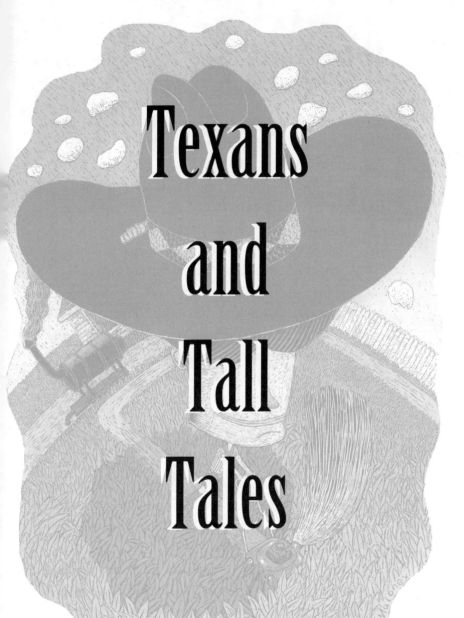

Texans
and
Tall
Tales

Out-of-staters may laugh at Texans, but never as hard as we laugh at ourselves. Perhaps that is because non-Texans may actually buy into the Texas stereotypes, whereas we natives recognize both the absurdity and the irony of them. One theory of Texas humor history holds that the Texas brag sprang up in the mid-nineteenth century as a response to the sheer unlivability of the land. To counteract bad reports from new settlers to their families back home, worried speculators conjured up outrageous claims about the golden land, claiming that the soil was so rich that it took two boys just to lug a single ear of corn.

Newspaper editors also took up the cause with gusto, asserting that, when harvest rolled around, farmers simply whistled up a cyclone to blow the kernels off the cobs and whisk them directly into the barn. Later, Texas brags grew more elaborate and detailed: according to one, if all the hogs in Texas were one giant hog, it could dig the Panama Canal with three roots and a grunt, and if all the steers in Texas were one giant steer, it could stand with its front feet in the Gulf of Mexico, its hind feet in Hudson Bay, and punch a hole in the moon with its horns while brushing the mist off the aurora borealis with its tail.

Inevitably, the Texas brag became intertwined with the tall tale, which evolved largely independently among Texas cowboys as a campfire comedy routine. Faced at day's end with a distinct lack of entertainment choices, they took turns spinning far-fetched yarns for the amusement of their fellow cowpokes.

Many bragfests glorified a single stellar cowhand, such as the lanky, legendary Pecos Bill—the all-time-tallest Texan. According to western lore, Pecos Bill (named for the West Texas river) could ride a mountain lion, rope a tornado, and drown a rattlesnake by spitting in its eye. He also taught his pet prairie dogs to dig the postholes for his fences, and carried a huge gun; it was so big that, when a sandstorm hit, he could just run up the barrel for shelter.

By the 1930s, Texas oilmen had created a similar Paul-Bunyan-like hero for their industry: Gib Morgan, who drilled his wells so deep that once a roughneck fell in and tumbled all the way to China, where he was rescued. The man sent back a cable assuring Morgan that "She's making 10,000 barrels a day at this end, too."

The Texas joke evolved from both the brag and the tall tale, emphasizing at least one aspect of all things Texan. Funny man Bennett Cerf, among others, included a chapter on "The Texas Joke" in one of his collections. An underlying assumption was the enviability of being Texan. The basic Texas-pride joke runs along the lines of "Never ask a man what state he's from. If he's a Texan, he'll tell you soon enough; if he's not, there's no use embarrassing him."

During the '50s and '60s, most Texas stories revolved around the staggering size of crops, critters, bank accounts, and everything else. Humorist Boyce House, a longtime Waco newspaper columnist, once explained that Texans put bells on their children so they can hear when the plane-size hawks try to snatch up the kids and carry them away. In an extension of this joke, a man boasted that he threw a rock to kill a hawk with a 50-foot wingspan—to which a listener replied, "Hmm—must have been a young 'un."

Weather was, and still is, an especially popular topic. Panhandlers like to note that when Admiral Peary reached the North Pole, he remarked "Gee, I'll bet it's cold in Amarillo this morning." A Yankee, visiting Houston in the August heat, comments quizzically, "You mean to tell me that folks live here when there ain't no war?" And a belovedly hoary line is that of an anonymous West Texas farmer: "I wish it would rain. Not for my sake, because I've seen it rain, but on account of my 10-year-old son."

Ignorance, too, was a common theme in the Texas joke. For example, a vacationing Yankee comments to a cowboy, "Awfully rainy today—like the Flood." "The Flood?" repeats the cowboy. "Yes, the Flood," the Yankee repeats impatiently. "You know—Noah, the Ark, Mount Ararat." "Well," the cowboy says, "I haven't read the paper yet this morning."

Texans ribbed tenderfeet in turn for their reverse ignorance. Case in point: A cowboy says to a dude-ranch guest, "What kind of saddle do you want—with a horn or without?" Replies the dude: "Without, I guess—there doesn't seem to be much traffic out here."

Two Texas cartoonists built their careers on such humor. Ace Reid of Kerrville, whose sketchy panels graced many a small-town bank calendar, created the bumbling duo Zeb and Jake; a typical panel shows Jake pinned beneath his horse and the longhorn he was trying to rope, as Zeb drawls, "It looks serious, Jake, but it ain't hopeless."

C. M. Rogers of Austin created a series of risque '50s-era "boast" cards, such as one showing two curvy wanna-be cowgirls clutching their outsize rears, which are radiating stars and ache lines; the picture is captioned, "Why do they call it tender*foot*?"

Poverty, a way of life for some farmers, was leavened with lines such as "The corn's pretty poor this year. We had some for dinner last night, and Pa ate 14 acres." Conversely, the sheer toughness of plants and animals provided fodder, too. Another farmer story tells of a prize hog who somehow got hold of a stick of dynamite and began chewing on it. The hog's owner later complained to a neighbor: "The dynamite blew up, broke both the windows in the house, flattened the barn, and killed all the chickens. And you know, I've got a mighty sick hog on my hands, too."

Finally, morality (as always) provides a rich lode to mine. One joke tells of a small-town newspaper editor who was short of material one week, so he printed the full text of the Ten Commandments on the front page. He soon received a note from a local rancher that read, "Cancel my subscription. You're getting too damned personal."

As the era of excess waned, the jokes about bigness and richness did, too—arguably because John F. Kennedy's death had made Texas clichés seem a lot less funny. The Dallas assassination reshaped America's perception of Texans from loaded-with-cash funny to loaded-with-bullets scary. The state's maturation into an increasingly urban and sophisticated place helped, too.

Local wags cast about for a successor to the Texas joke and found a target long favored by University of Texas' many alumni: a main UT rival, the Aggies, whose moniker came from the full name of their alma mater, Texas A&M [Agricultural and Mechanical] University in College Station, Texas. Soon A&M's diverse student population had been condensed into a single type—the hopeless hayseed who's dumb as a bag of hair. In a typical joke, an Aggie brags that he finished a jigsaw puzzle in only two months—even though the box clearly stated "three to five years."

Aggies may have the last laugh, however, as A&M is Texas' top university in many ways. Its admission criteria are demanding, its graduate programs include the state's finest veterinarian school, and its faculty boasts Nobel prize-winning scientists. In spite of the university's outstanding credentials, the Aggie joke still reigns as Texas' most revered form of regional humor. Ultimately, though, the joke is on us.

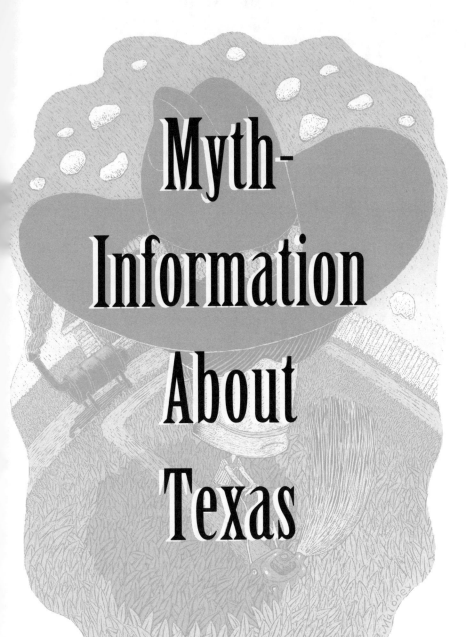

Myth-
Information
About
Texas

Of all the myths about Texas, few are called for but many are chosen. Not just our fellow Americans but people all over the world cling to their long-cherished beliefs about the state—that Texans are all cowboys, for instance, or that the land is all flat and flat-out ugly. But modern Texas is a far cry from the stereotypes perpetrated over the years by the silver screen and the comic postcard.

We Texans may object to the errors—at least the ones we don't like—but we can't exactly protest them; after all, we ourselves have fostered the tall tale and the Texas brag (as well as their modern offshoot, the chamber of commerce). Although I have "myth apprehensions" about incurring the wrath of my fellow Texans, I declare many of Texas' most legendary myths to be false. In the interest of truthfulness, I say, let's knock 'em flat on their assumptions.

MYTH NUMBER ONE:
TEXANS ARE FRIENDLY

This is a fine how-do-you-do, but we're no longer welcoming and often barely civil. The proof is on any stretch of city freeway: rush hour is hell on wheels. Maybe this highway hostility springs from overcrowding—after all, the love of wide-open spaces is wired into the DNA of Texans, even third-generation urbanites. We believe in herding cattle, not cars. It's possible that the automotive stampede is the result of pure machismo, although women drivers are just as reckless and aggressive as men.

Perhaps the cause is simply the security of anonymity; on the freeway, not only are we traveling in the midst of strangers but we also often drive behind tinted glass, which cuts down on the glare—and the glares.

Back before freeways—when interstates were just a mirage on the horizon of life's blacktop—Texans wended their way down two-lane roads at reasonable speeds and delighted in meeting fellow motorists. Typically, such drivers offered the "hi" sign—a quick, polite lifting of the index finger of either hand on the wheel. Today, that finger is not the one most likely to be raised.

Texans also like size, in vehicles and everything else (see myth number two)—so their beloved pickup trucks and sport utility vehicles have become the Brahma bulls of the four-lane, easily cowing cute little heifer-size Japanese cars. In Texas, many drivers feel the same kind of disdain for economy cars that a cowboy feels for a mule.

Finally, Texas is so gosh-darn big that drivers feel compelled to travel at over-the-top speeds to minimize car time. (As a '40s-era postcard verse put it, "The sun has riz/The sun has set/And here I is/In Texas yet.") This long-haul mentality applies even to suburban residents who face a mere 45-minute drive, but try to shave off a minute or two by fighting far with fire. Newcomers, take note: Natives always convey distance in hours—not miles. For example, if asked how far it is from Houston to Dallas, a Texan will reply, "Oh, about three and a half hours."

Urban Texans drive unfriendly. There's the cuttinsky, who nearly clips your car as he abruptly pulls in front, then gestures obscenely if you honk in protest. There's the me-first moron, who dawdles along well below the posted limit until you try to pass him, at which point he speeds up to parallel you. There's the rule-bender, whose scofflaw habits include using the exit lane to pass on the right—to the detriment of others in his pathological path.

There's also the ever-annoying tail-gater, whose valuable time you are wasting by failing to match his pace. You can daydream about taking action—stopping short, bracing for the crash, and then saying sweetly, "That's the brakes!"—but try to resist the temptation. Many Texans carry guns, and you could land yourself in a large-caliber mess.

Whatever the reason *for* our street madness, there's no reason *to* it. In losing our, shall we say, motor skills, we have also lost our social skills. The name of our state comes from the language of the Caddo Indians, in which "tejas" meant "friend." Note that there are no longer any Caddoes hereabouts. Wonder if they also had a word for "jerk"?

MYTH NUMBER TWO: EVERYTHING'S BIGGER IN TEXAS

Sizing up the origin of this myth is easy. Texas was, for more than a century, the nation's biggest state. Before that, while still an independent republic, it was even larger, covering parts of what are now New Mexico,

Colorado, Kansas, and Wyoming. Naturally, this point of pride had mass appeal for the home folks, who felt somewhat inferior to more venerable bastions of civilization such as Virginia and New York.

Inevitably, they began applying superlatives to more attributes than merely Texas' mass. This fed regional folklore (a word that essentially means "lies that everybody tells"), which began to record equally outsized phenomena such as the giant jackrabbit—a two-ton critter capable of being saddled and ridden or strung up and fileted, depending on whether a cowboy needed to be seated or sated.

A popular postcard of the day was the "Texan's Map of the World," showing a swollen Texas dominating the U.S., with lesser states squashed in and given hardy-har-har names like "Lose-iana" and "Pencil-vania." A former governor, Pat Neff, once claimed that "Rhode Island would scarcely make a watch fob for Texas."

Newspaper columnist Boyce House, who reigned as Texas' chief humorist during the '40s, bragged that "Texas is so huge that if you used the northern line of the Panhandle for a hinge, you'd put Brownsville so close to the Arctic Circle that the Mexican hot tamale peddlers could exchange their wares with the Eskimos for polar bear steaks." He also said, "If all the mules in Texas could be made into one mule, he could kick the 'man' out of the moon. If all the bales of cotton grown in Texas could be made into one stack, you would have a stairway reaching to the pearly gates."

Then came a day that will live in infamy: January 3, 1959, when the nation welcomed its 49th state, Alaska. Twice as big (and a lot colder) than Texas, Alaska quickly froze out many of our claims to fame. Whereas once Texans wallowed in superiority, they suddenly found themselves reeling from the number-two label, a status they had previously regarded as a pile of, well, number two. Alaska's statehood also necessitated altering one line of the state song, from "biggest and grandest," to "boldest and grandest."

The intervening decades have lessened the shock a bit but, ultimately, when Alaska outsized Texas, it caused a subtle reconfiguring of Texans' bravado. They regrouped, drew on the never-say-die attitude of their hardy pioneer ancestors, and transferred their beloved hyperbole from success to excess. By poking fun at themselves and not at others, they could still enjoy the brag and at the same time salve their wounded pride. In modern Texas, bragging is a culturally approved cure for the blues.

Despite our fondness for bigness (good *or* bad), sometimes it's the little things we're proudest of. The Alamo, for example, has a larger-than-life reputation, and valor was clearly its defenders' forte. But the building itself, which sits in the middle of downtown San Antonio, looks downright insignificant. An even smaller claim to fame for Texas is the silicon chip, invented in 1958 by Jack Kilby, an engineer for Texas Instruments in Dallas. It might not be the most popular chip in Texas—that would be the tostada—but it sure lasts a lot longer.

MYTH NUMBER THREE: TEXAS IS FLAT

This misconception exists for two major reasons: interstates and entertainment. U.S. highways cut through the state at its flattest, most geographically uninteresting areas, which makes things speedier for both road builders and road users. I-35, for example, traverses the state from the border city of Laredo north through San Antonio, Austin, Waco, and Dallas-Fort Worth before entering Oklahoma. I-10 runs east-west from Orange, on the Louisiana line, to El Paso, which is practically in New Mexico.

Both highways are apparently interminable, long enough to make motorists—particularly out-of-staters—feel they have been traveling since the the Dead Sea was only sick. That and the unremarkable countryside that flanks both freeways gives many passers-through a bad first impression. The solution is to detour onto state highways, which criss-cross the most scenic pockets of Texas: the Hill Country, full of limestone boulders and twisty roads; East Texas, replete with tall pines and swampy atmosphere; the dune-dotted coastline, all 367 miles of it; and rugged Big Bend, at once beautiful and severe.

For residents of smaller states, the sheer size of Texas is hard to comprehend. I once tried to explain to a complaining New Jerseyite, who had followed I-40 across the Panhandle, that parts of Texas were in fact quite pretty. She eyed me in disbelief and explained slowly, as if to the village idiot, "But I've driven through it." (Of course, she thought the Panhandle *was* Texas! Her entire state isn't much bigger than some of our counties.)

Many misguided movies also underscore the common belief that all of Texas is all parched prairies or mountainous wilderness. Westerns were particularly indifferent to inaccuracies. A western starring Roy Rogers, *The Song of Texas* (1943), featured a ring of snow-capped peaks the likes of which can't be found south of Colorado.

The great director John Ford, for another example, loved Monument Valley, which straddles Arizona and Utah and features towers of ultra-rugged, wind-carved rock and an air of bleak menace. Several of his classic films were shot there, including *The Searchers* (1956)—though its setting is presented unapologetically as Texas. *Walk on the Wild Side* (1962) committed a different sort of topographical goof—it relocated a swath of West Texas desert to sticky Beaumont. Envision the effect of rattlesnakes denning in bank drive-throughs, javelinas having a latte, and tarantulas toodling around downtown. Now *there's* some movie material. At any rate, this brings us to:

MYTH NUMBER FOUR:
TEXAS IS THE WILD WEST

Other cinematic liberties also color much of Hollywood's Texas-themed movies. Filmmakers, for example, were stuck on saguaro cactus, which doesn't grow as far east as Texas, but its dramatic silhouette was too good to resist. They also liked to Texify sagebrush, another Arizona plant. Although the famous outlaw Billy the Kid actually used New Mexico as his stomping grounds, native son Audie Murphy played the young gunslinger as a Lone Star boy in *The Kid From Texas* (1950), because the name "Texas" conveys far more grit and glory than do the names of most other locales.

Early cowboy star Tom Mix was born in Pennsylvania, but his studio bio once claimed he was a Texas Ranger from El Paso. And speaking of the Texas Rangers, scores of movies set in Texas drew on the time-honored cowboy-and-Indian conflict to liven up the plot; the truth is, however, that soon after the Civil War the Rangers had chased most tribes out of the eastern half of Texas, and within a decade all but the Quahadi Comanches had moved to Oklahoma reservations or to the happy hunting grounds in the sky. Today, only the Tigua Indians, who live near El Paso, and the Alabama-Coushatta tribe, in East Texas near the Big Thicket, remain.

MYTH NUMBER FIVE:
TEXANS ARE BACKWARD AND IGNORANT

Well, not all of us are. Most of us *can* be backward from time to time—whenever we're not facing forward, in fact. The hillbilly appellation, however, is false, like all generalizations. This myth persists because early Anglo settlers in Texas often lived in squalor and poverty, as did pioneers everywhere else. Also, range cowboys were the carefree bachelors of the nineteenth century, often thoroughly insulated from civilization and womenfolk; the flip side of the taciturn, white-hatted hero was the awkward, stumbling bumpkin who aw-shucked over newfangled inventions like the telephone and stuttered in godawful girl-shyness.

Many Depression-era photographers traveled through Texas to document migrant workers and hard times as part of Franklin D. Roosevelt's make-work projects. These hollow-cheeked, sunken-eyed subjects, unfortunately, added to the white-trash-Texan image.

Finally, from the turn of the century through the '60s, the discovery of oil fueled overnight boomtowns statewide practically overnight, and many hard-scrabble farmers harvested a bumper crop of mineral rights. These instant millionaires were quickly stereotyped as local yokels who squandered their windfall on Cadillacs to park by the hog trough and on mink overalls to clothe their passel of brats.

Naturally, these stories sprang from those folks who weren't lucky enough to hit a gusher themselves. In 1958, when Kilgore native Van Cliburn won the prestigious Moscow International Piano Competition, music lovers worldwide marveled that such an artistic genius could come out of [gasp, blink] Texas! This regional bias still persists today: Texas political analysts fretted that George W. Bush's Texas governorship would hurt his chances at the presidency.

After World War II, Texas' population was, for the first time, more urban than rural, but the poor-and-rustic image persisted. At age 10, I lived in Ohio for a year, and my fellow fourth-graders, upon discovering that I was from Texas, asked me if I owned a ranch, if I rode a horse, and (my favorite) if I had to fetch water. Sure—from the sink, like everybody else.

Also adding to the clodhopper stereotype is the Texas drawl, which many residents come by honestly and others enjoy borrowing for humorous effect, particularly when snooty Yankees are around. For many Northeasterners, an exaggerated Texas accent has a nails-squeaking-on-a-blackboard effect, rendering them incapable of noticing that they're being ribbed.

While "Foat Wuth, I Luv Yew" was once a popular bumper sticker, Fort Worth residents, along with the rest of us, are perfectly capable of pronouncing their R's when they so choose. Another oft-mangled phrase is "barbed wire," which is usually said just like it looks unless a buzz-saw-voiced Brooklynite is holding forth within earshot, in which case any native Texan will immediately make it "bob war" just as a barb.

MYTH NUMBER SIX:
TEXANS ARE WEALTHY

Wrong, darn it. In fact, Texas' per-capita income is consistently below the national average. This is another myth pumped up by boomtown lore. A typical hokey cartoon of the '50s depicted two millionaires haggling over who should buy a helicopter. One prevails by saying, "Let me get this, George—you bought lunch." Another showed a lanky rancher reclining on bags of cash and overseeing his derrick-studded property. The caption reads "A Poor Texan." And odds are that, today, Texans who are rich got there by cashing in on something other than ranching or oil; of the 35 Texas companies on the 1999 *Fortune* 500 ranking of largest U.S. corporations, only a dozen are energy-related.

MYTH NUMBER SEVEN: TEXAS' WEATHER IS WORSE THAN ANY OTHER STATE'S

This, too, is hot air (or a snow job, if you'd prefer). Texas is simply big enough that there may be opposite kinds of weather affecting it all at once—a heat wave in the Valley, a dust storm in the Panhandle, and flooding in Central Texas—but plenty of states are hotter or cooler (temperature-wise, that is). Again, blame the brag and the tall tale. It's made us Texans rather weather-vain.

Creature
Discomforts

A whole herd of Texas animals are icons of the state and mascots to its residents, who have long distinguished between critters (good animals) and varmints (bad ones). Critters helped settle Texas when it was the wide-openest space in the Wild West; varmints hindered the state's civilization but nonetheless earned people's respect for their pure cussedness. Historically, though, the animals that early Texans tussled with were far different from those that typically test residents today.

THE LONGHORN

Arguably the best known animal symbol in Texas is the longhorn, whose distant ancestors were the Spanish cattle first introduced to the New World by explorers as far back as Christopher Columbus. Inevitably, a few cows and bulls hoofed it into the wild, where they promptly reproduced. The resultant untamed bovines were scrappy, rangy things whose impressive horn span commonly measured eight or nine feet.

Tales of 15-foot horns are of dubious authenticity; a common brag for a particularly well-endowed bull was that "it took a jaybird 48 hours to fly from horn to horn." According to another yarn, the reason the animal developed such massive horns was because, during severe droughts, they kept it from falling through deep cracks in creek beds.

Such folklore conveniently added to the everything's-bigger-in-Texas myth, but in fact the longhorn itself was a scrawny, slat-sided critter. Ranchers' big beef with the longhorn was its minor food value, compared to a hefty fat-packer like the Hereford. There were compensations, though; throughout the nineteenth century, the long-horn's chief virtue was its cost: free. Many a wannabe rancher simply tracked longhorns down and rounded them up—well, "simply" may be the wrong word, as long-horns were notoriously bad-tempered and didn't submit gracefully to capture.

By the 1900s, longhorns were almost extinct. In 1948, Sid Richardson, an oilman from Fort Worth, and J. Frank Dobie, a Texas folklorist emeritus from Austin, joined forces to resurrect the longhorn—scraping up enough donations to assemble a herd of sorts that they ensconced at Fort Griffin State Park near Albany. Subsquently, the breed slowly came back—mostly as a conversation piece, at first, but later as a legitimate breed properly styled the Longhorn, with a capital L.

Today, there's even a Texas Longhorn Breeders Association. But, by far, the most common and famous Longhorns of today are the University of Texas Longhorns. At football games and at other sport meets, loyal UT fans brandish the "Hook 'em, 'Horns" sign, cre-ated by extending the index finger and pinkie while holding down the other two fingers with the thumb.

THE RATTLESNAKE

Texas' best-known varmint (as opposed to critter) is the rattlesnake. Several species live within the state's boundaries, but the meanest of them all is the western diamondback, whose Latin name is *Crotalus atrox*; the "atrox" comes from the Latin word that also gave us "atrocious," and it certainly is—it accounts for some 90 percent of bites reported in the nation each year.

The western diamondback is not only mean and aggressive but big—the largest confirmed length in the state was seven feet, five inches—and thus it injects a proportionately larger, and more life-threatening, dose of venom: one strike and you're most likely out. Its warning sound—a gut-wrenching, adrenaline-producing clamor that sounds like marbles shaken in a tin cup—gives new meaning to the term "rattled."

Inevitably, Texas braggologists spun yarns about the rattlesnake. Texas Ranger Rip Ford claimed to have clashed with a 10-footer; regrettably, he lacked an eye-witness to the event. A famous tall tale about Pecos Bill, the Paul Bunyan of Texas, relates how that larger-than-lifesize cowboy used an even longer rattler to rope a pesky cougar.

Since rattlers are cold-blooded, stories abound about cowboys who, while sleeping under the stars during a trail drive or roundup, awakened to find themselves sharing their bedroll with a snake—an experience many modern Texas women can relate to.

Similarly, tales regularly crop up about various farming folk who, during cold weather, discovered a diamondback curled up on their pickup's engine to absorb its heat. That, of course, was the windshield viper.

THE FIRE ANT

Today, the average Texan isn't likely to cross horns with a Longhorn or a rattlesnake unless they're driving back roads or hiking remote paths. Instead, the usual

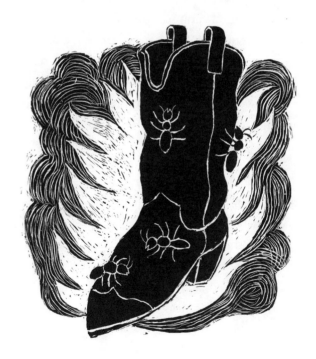

23

daily scourges are insects. Dreadful enough to eclipse the mosquito and the chigger is a relative newcomer, the fire ant (*Solenopsis invicta*)—a bitsy little insect whose size belies its viciousness. This dreaded antagonist arrived uninvited in the U.S. in the '30s and within 20 years had spread west to Texas and chowed down on its lesser antecedents.

Fire ants can also kill other insects, lizards, rodents, birds, and even fawns; swarms of hundreds of fire ants can fell allergic humans. Whatever the species of prey, the fire ant clamps down with its pincers, then uses its stinger to repeatedly inject the venom, whose burning effects gave the six-legged varmint its name.

The underground infestations of these ferocious little ants are revealed by large mounds, either flattened or rounded, that you might term anterooms; below may live as many as half a million potential flesh-arsonists. In Texas, enjoying the outdoors is no longer a picnic.

THE BAT

Equally nontraditional—but in a good way—is the bat. Austin boasts the largest urban bat colony in the world. Some three-quarters of a million of the creatures live under the immense Congress Avenue bridge near Austin's downtown, and the city—which originally considered the bats a nuisance—eventually came to embrace them as a tourist attraction.

Between April and October, visitors and residents alike gather at dusk to watch the bats emerge in a long, smokelike swirl to chow down on mosquitoes and other airborne bugs. (Pity the fire ant doesn't fly, eh?)

The exact species found in Austin is the Mexican free-tailed bat—and observers, be warned: when they're flying overhead, they're especially free-tailed. If you're not careful, you might get nailed with bat guano. Austinites, who have become batty for their bats, easily throw about terms like "echo location," the term for the critters' radarlike communication. So many locals are conversant with such lingo that you might call their newfound knowledge "echo locution."

THE HORNY TOAD

This endearingly ugly little reptile is properly termed the horned lizard, but native Texans call it the horny toad. The "horny" in question refers to its spikes and spines, which protect it against snakes, raptors, and other predators; despite the name, the horny toad mates only once a year.

Although it is rather chaste, however, it is no longer chased: Whereas once the horny toad was a common backyard resident, a small pet-at-large, today it is relatively uncommon. The combination of steady urbanization and the widespread use of pesticides have so reduced its numbers that the species is now protected and known to most children only through pictures. Nonetheless, it remains a totem—make that "toadem"—for Texans today.

THE ARMADILLO

This primitive-looking mammal has much in common with the horny toad. It, too, is charmingly unattractive and boasts a built-in defense system—in this case, an exterior of overlapping bony plates that allows it to curl into a ball and foil attackers (the word "armadillo," in fact, means "little armored one" in Spanish). But the armadillo can be a pest; its compulsive burrowing has riddled many a yard or garden with unsightly and dangerous holes.

The armadillo's adoption as a Texas symbol can be traced to artist Jim Franklin, who featured them in a series of comic and surreal posters for the late great Armadillo World Headquarters—a counterculture music venue in Austin, and then later for Lone Star Beer. Texas drivers commonly spot the armadillo along the highway, where it is the state's number-one source of roadkill. For both its pesky habits and its victimization by vehicle, we might rechristen it the "harmadillo."

THE ROADRUNNER

Speaking of car versus critter, the roadrunner—which favors dry, empty country—is the only Texas animal who can take on the automobile and win. When startled by an oncoming car, the roadrunner takes off not into the brush but down the road, in apparent "wanna drag" mode. The closer the vehicle gets, the faster the bird runs, only to veer off at the last minute into the nearest field or thicket.

Note: the roadrunner *can* fly, but only for short hops; it prefers to travel by land. Regardless of what its cartoon counterpart may say, the real roadrunner doesn't go "beep beep"—its cry is more of a muted "kook kook," which is probably what he considers most of us humans to be.

THE COYOTE

Another varmint enshrined in the pop culture pantheon, the real coyote is far from the misnamed Wile E. Coyote of Warner Bros. cartoon fame. Unlike that hapless animated creature, the real coyote is plenty intelligent; he knows better than to target the roadrunner—although almost all other smaller critters are fair game.

In a stereotypical southwestern image, the coyote has his head thrown back, howling at the moon. This overused image has inspired some truly dreadful arts and crafts (which inspire howling of a different sort), but in reality, the coyote is more likely to yap or yip.

Although the coyote continues to plague ranchers by preying on livestock, the word has come to mean something far scarier and dangerous in human terms: a *coyote* is also the person who, for a fee, helps illegal aliens cross the Mexican border into the U.S.—usually across desolate landscape, and often to their deaths. *This* coyote is truly the beast.

In Texas, Even the Plants Have Claws

In Texas, you can stop and smell the flowers, but you may regret it—the Lone Star State's flora, like its fauna, is apt to attack. Texas bull nettle, for instance, which grows all over the state, has blossoms that smell sweet but leaves that are covered with tiny stinging hairs; it's also called "tread-softly" and, in Mexico, malo mujer or "bad woman."

Devil's claw, an unpleasantly scented wild herb, produces a woody-shelled seed pod that, when dry, splits down the middle; the stem then curls into curved talons which hook onto unfortunate four- or two-legged passersby. As a reminder for residents and a warning for transplants, following are the dossiers for three of Texas' toughest plants.

PRICKLY PEAR

As early explorers and settlers learned, living in cactus land is not for the spineless. For instance, cholla, a shrubby West Texas variety, has thick, fleshy stems that bristle with inch-long spines. Ocotillo (not strictly a cactus, for the botanical purists with us) has spurlike protrusions that also have hypodermic qualities.

That prickly pair are, however, not the most common cacti in the state. That would be *Opuntia lindheimeri*, better known as prickly pear, which should literally be handled with kid gloves. It's not only studded with a daunting number of obvious spines but also with tiny, almost invisible spinelets called glochids, which are equally sharp and almost impossible to remove. Many a wannabe naturalist has discovered this fact the hard way, by approaching the cactus ungloved, usually to pick the small, plum-like fruits, which are also spiny (hence the cactus's common name).

The fruits of this cactus—properly called *tunas*, a Spanish word that sounds fishy to us English-speakers—are purplish-pink when ripe and often used to flavor jelly and candy. Also edible are the pads themselves, which have a

sort of green-bean flavor and often appear in Mexican-style salads. As a vegetable it's called *nopal* and is common in Texas produce stands; before you buy it, just be sure it's been de-spined, so no pall is cast over your meal.

The Mesquite

The mesquite is a shrubby little tree that is deeply rooted in Texas culture. For Native American nomads and early settlers, the tree was in many ways a blessing— its creamy blossoms attracted honeybees; its sweet-tasting beans fattened livestock; and, on the plains, its fragrant hardwood often proved the sole source for kindling and fenceposts.

For all its benefits, however, mesquite extracted its pound of flesh, or at least its spot of blood, by means of nasty thumb-long thorns. And the mesquite's slender, feathery look belies its toughness; a sort of prairie iceberg, the tree itself conceals roots reaching as far down as sixty feet. The mesquite is a metaphor for Texans: user-friendly, but prepared to defend itself; able to thrive in dryness and desolation; and unwilling to part easily from its native soil.

The Sticker Burr

Under the law of the land, the sticker burr is a common criminal—a stick-up artist, at best. Unlike prickly pear and mesquite, which prefer wild and open terrain, for the sticker burr the grass is always greener. It likes to lurk in apparently velvety lawns, but does not disdain to invade untended lots as well.

Its host plant, a weed masquerading as a grass, insinuates itself amid pleasanter yard carpetings and waits until its spiny seeds harden into tiny torture machines—a maturing process that takes place in the summer when it can target the highest percentage of tender tootsies. Even the feistiest young Texans know that wearing shoes is the only answer; even being shod in sandals is shoddy protection. In time-honored kid fashion, however, many still insist on going barefoot—the little masochists. It's their way of saying "stick it" to the tiny nemesis invading their turf.

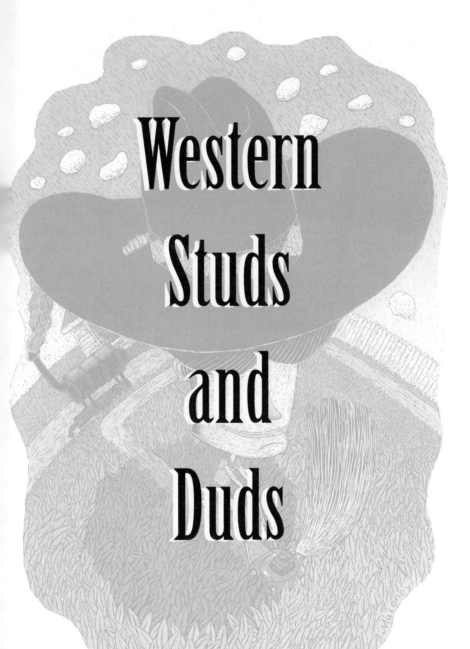

Western
Studs
and
Duds

We Texans love our western heritage. Images of rugged cowboys, trail drives, rearing horses, and such persuade us to buy western-inspired food, clothes, and practically everything else. But the fact is, real cowboys—though greatly admired—are a distinct minority in the state today. Most of us are far from, and a far cry from, the rugged Marlboro-man types depicted on billboards and in Hollywood miniseries. This Texas stereotype persists even though Texas has been a largely urban state for almost 50 years.

Modern Texans wear business suits and button-downs, pantyhose and pumps (sometimes all at once—but that's another story). But despite our urbanness—or, arguably, our urbanity—we still enjoy donning the trappings and trimmings of the cowpoke from time to time. Like the Scots, who generally eschew kilts for daily wear, we save our Texas togs for special occasions. (It almost kilt you to read that, didn't it?) Today the western wardrobe—jeans, boots, belts, and hats—has essentially become our national costume, and when we do dress up, we aren't playing around.

The most essential item of Texas fashion gear is a pair of jeans. In fact, a pair of jeans is possibly the single most de rigueur piece of clothing in the entire universe—a testament to the heroic power of the cowboy myth. Brand-name blue jeans are still a black-market luxury in much of the world.

If working cowboys had to choose a brand of jeans, it would probably be Wrangler (with that name, how could

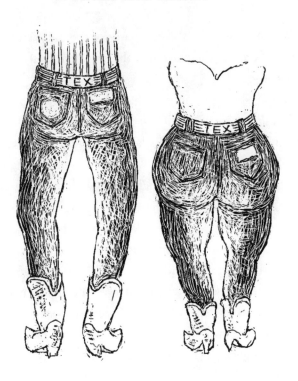

they resist?). Others go the Lee way. Levi's—probably the label with the greatest international name recognition— seems to be a top choice for non-cowboys. Many haute couture and knock-off versions exist, however—they were bound to, given the popularity of denim over the last quarter-century or so.

For national-costume occasions—such as barbecues, rodeos, and San Jacinto Day—western-cut jeans are preferred. You can spot authentic cowboys in the crowd by the washed-to-death hue of their pants (dark denim is an off-and-on fad), the slightly bow-legged waddle, the worn insides of the thighs (marks of the habitual rider), and, of course, the outline of the snuff can in their back pocket.

Cowgirls exhibit more fashion daring—they don jeans in a rainbow of colors. Their pants are not just snug, like their menfolk's, but cling like Saran Wrap to Jell-O. On a curvy cowgirl, the effect is more neck-wrenching than a bullrider's spill. Even rancherettes with more, er, corn-fed haunches opt to wear their Wranglers skin-tight. Their fellas, God love 'em, don't mind a bit: Remember, most cowboys spend a lot of time staring at the south end of northbound Herefords.

Another essential component of the Texas national costume is a pair of boots—western boots, that is. Cowboys are a notoriously underpaid group, but as far as footwear goes, they insist on being well-heeled—on wear-ing boots made not just for walking but for hooking onto stirrups for horse control. The traditional pointed toe, a design feature often attributed to pioneer bootmaker H. J. Justin, allows the boot to slip easily out of the stirrup; the distinctive stacked heels provide sure-footedness, as well as a free built-in defense against fresh cow patties, and the extra inches contribute to that classic tall-Texan look and swagger.

Depending on what part of the state you're in, the tra-ditional pointed-toe boot design may be regarded as an absolute necessity, a retro fashion statement, or a hope-lessly outdated look. Yet another point of view comes from Texas editor and Uvalde native Jane Dure, who notes that "pointy toes are for Sunday," and further points out the current popularity of the rounded toe, usually on the shorty, sporty boots called ropers.

One basic pair of brown or black boots with conservatively matching stitching will sew up your boot needs for years, maybe decades, if you save them for special occasions. But the genre comes in an amazing variety of colors, including pink. A pastel pair like that gathers dust in the back of my closet 364 days a year. But on the 365th day, I feel like Dale Evans all day long. (Folkloric footnote: when you're wearing boots that color, you pronounce it "pank".)

There is an impressive spectrum of leathers, to boot, including ostrich, snake, and elephant; these classy choices are the favorite of Houston businessmen, the boot-wearingest of urban Texans. The spiffiest boots of all may be Luccheses (Loo-KAY-sees), named for the Italian brothers who brought their family's skill at leatherworking to San Antonio in the 1880s.

Most of us, however, are perfectly content with less expensive but equally admirable boots, including Justins (named for the pointy-toe-ologist) and Tony Lamas, the namesake footgear of El Paso's famous bootmeister. Brand aside, the popularity of boots in Texas is a shoo-in.

Tradition requires that you top off the Texas national costume with a cowboy hat. As with boots, the choices are staggering. The crown can be low or high, creased or uncreased. An especially high, usually uncreased crown is one like that favored by Hoss Cartwright on the vintage western *Bonanza* (played by Dan Blocker, a native Texan). It's also called a ten-gallon hat, an exaggeration, of course, and also a mangling of Spanish. In the late nineteenth century, a particularly fancy hat had a lot of *galón,* or braid, on it, and American cowboys borrowed the style and the word from their Mexican counterparts.

A hat with a low crown is pretty low on the Texas style list, since it lends a certain suggestion of Southern gambler rather than western hero. A medium-high crown is most common. A lot of drugstore cowboys today prefer tietack-like pins to braid or ribbon for hat decor. These crown jewels, so to speak, usually depict a favored beer, car, critter, or Texas icon.

The typical hat emporium is also brimming with brim choices. Most Texans prefer a wide brim. For rodeo performers and professional working hands, the front and back of the brim tend to curve down, a result of being yanked tight on the wearer's head to thwart high winds or hyperactive mounts. Narrow or rolled brims tend to broadcast your citified origins.

As for material, there are really only two choices: felt and straw. The difference is seasonal. Wear a felt hat any time between April and October and the difference will be felt, all right. That material is for cooler weather, but even a winter-only hat soon develops its own distinctive sweat stain. Straw is a summerweight material; it not only reduces glare but also keeps the wearer cool, no matter how hot-headed he may be.

Optional accessories for playing cowboy include the bandana, the western-style shirt, the big buckle, and the name belt. Once printed solely in the time-honored solid-red or -blue paisley print, the bandana has gone upscale, in part because it is now associated with farmers more than ranchers (and never make the mistake of confusing the two—farmers raise plants, ranchers raise animals). Today, bandanas come in patriotic Texas prints, such as bluebonnets or branding irons, but still protect the wearer from dust if he's riding herd—or from recognition, if he's robbing a bank.

As for the western-style shirt, there are certain must-haves. One is faux mother-of-pearl snaps, which are sturdier than buttons and less likely to snag on, say, a steer horn; instead, they pop open in a snap, which makes it easier for cowboys to extricate themselves from danger (or, if someone else needs help, to give you the shirt off their back).

Another design essential on the western shirt is a yoke, front and back; a third is breast pockets; and a fourth is long sleeves—anything less would be a shortcoming. Extra frou-frou like fringe and embroidery are a Hollywood embellishment that, in a life-imitates-art reversal, were soon adopted by rodeo riders as well; today, they often mark dude-ranch duds or Saturday-night show-offs.

The "name" belt, too, is an entertainment flourish. Typically the wearer's name—Tex, Slim, Red—is tooled

into the back of the belt. Corporate flacks should consider the untapped advertising potential here. A name
belt could exhort passersby to "Drink Coca-Cola!," or
implore them to "Please Don't Litter," assert a warning
like "Back Off!," or prevent heartbreak with "I'm
Married."

On the opposite side of the name belt message is the
bigger-than-Dallas buckle—another loan from the rodeo
world, where solid-gold or silver buckles, engraved with
names, dates, and wins, often serve as prizes. Such a
buckle provides quick cash in a pinch, as well as limited
protection in a fight. Some are so elaborately engraved
that only a close study can reveal the delicate details.
Hell-raising types are prone to asking good-looking
women to admire their buckle. Given its location, the
ladies are hard-pressed not to blush.

Beehive
Madness

Women in Texas apply the big-buckle syndrome to their hairstyles. They love excesses of tresses. They wig out over big hair. Why? One theory is that a mane of teased, frizzed, or flowing locks makes your hips look smaller, an especially important consideration for those ladies who like skin-tight jeans.

A second explanation derives from Texas' position as the buckle of the Bible Belt, where, for a good century

and a half, men were men and women were decoration; thus a woman's hair, the crowning glory decreed by Scripture, confirms her feminine virtue.

Finally, many women think the bigger or longer or curlier the hair, the younger-looking the face. There are more than a few wrinkles, however, in that version of big-hair-ology. For one thing, as we age, our various body parts tend to head south, so lanky hair only draws the eye downward, emphasizing the sag factor.

This factor explains why many older ladies, particularly in small towns sculpt their hair upward, preferably as high as possible. While older ladies often find beehives bedazzling (think of former governor Ann Richards' ivory tower); younger ones tend to be regional Rapunzels, favoring the carpet-size shag that Farrah Fawcett popularized in the '70s.

The biggest "don't" for either 'do is: don't leave it natural. Texas wind and weather (and today, even the usual gale-force-level car air-conditioning) can ravage ringlets like a tonsorial Torquemada. While Plains Indian women of centuries past used buffalo grease, the contemporary solution is hair spray—lots of hair spray, applied till every individual hair resists the pull of gravity. (During the inaugural festivities for Governor Richards in 1992, a giant papier-mâché can of hair spray joined the parade.) In his song "Northeast Texas Women," Willis Alan Ramsey refers to "cotton candy hair"—and certainly the stickiness factor is the same.

Quite a few female Texans also seem to prefer big bosoms. In 1998, the American Society of Plastic and Reconstructive Surgeons, who keep abreast of such matters, revealed that more breast-implant patients in Texas request the largest implants available than do women anywhere else. Like big hair, big chests help to minimize your hips and maximize your sex appeal. Just be considerate of the ever-suffering Texas independent oilman, and don't use the term "bust."

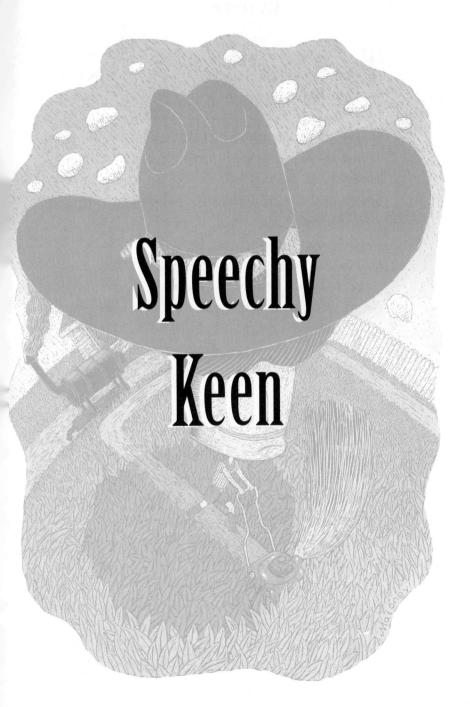

Speechy Keen

Texas idiom is full of charming, colorful, and corny say-ings—more so than any other state, not only because of Texas' size and geographical diversity but also because its heritage is equal parts Old South and Wild West, and it mines both of these rich verbal lodes.

"Texpressions" arise from a variety of disciplines. Chief among them is, perhaps, politics. Sam Rayburn, the long-time, storied Speaker of the House, was fond of admon-ishing his staff, "Don't count the crop before it's in the barn." Lyndon Baines Johnson once described wearing a tight pair of pants as "just like riding a wire fence."

Sportsmen as well as statesmen are great sources: Darrell Royal, football coach extraordinaire, was renowned for his ruralisms. He once bewildered the press corps by claiming a certain play was "harder than burn-ing a red elephant." Only years later did a journalist ask him to explain the phrase, which, to Royal's amusement, had been misheard; he had actually said "harder than burning a wet elephant."

The oil business, too, has given Texans a gusher of good sayings, but few, alas, are clean enough to print. Many others are westernisms that have survived well past the heyday of the cowboy. "A real pear-burner," for example, means a go-getter or a hard worker, and refers to the old-timey practice of burning the spines off prick-ly-pear pads to feed cattle during a drought.

Texas literature also offers many nuggets as well; in *All the Pretty Horses*, author Cormac McCarthy muses that "Scared money can't win, and a worried man can't love."

The majority of Texas sayings, however, come from anonymous men and women who managed to maintain their sense of humor, come hell or high water. That's how we modern Texans have come to inherit pithy little lines like the difference between "naked" and "nekkid": *Naked* means "no clothes on," and *nekkid* means "no clothes on and up to something."

For new Texans who want to sound like natives and for long-timers who want to expand their repertoire, read on to learn more Texas sayings—or, to put it another way: "Keep your fork. There's pie."

ANGRY

That really ruffles my tail feathers.

I'll have your guts for garters.

I'll fix your wagon.

I'd like to rid the ground of his shadow.

I'd like to put a rattlesnake in his pocket and ask him for a match.

I'm so mad I could jump up and down and spit golden b.b.'s.

She tore off a strip about it.

She could cuss the skin off a cat.

She got up on the wrong side of the sty.

He had a conniption fit.

He had a hissy fit.

He looks like somebody stole his clothes while he was swimming.

Tail up and stinger ready.

BAD, MEAN

He's one sick puppy, and we're downwind from the kennel.

He'd spoil if you kept him in the icebox.

He couldn't get along with the devil himself.

He and the devil drink through the same straw.

He ain't worth a bucket under a bull.

He could raise five dollars' worth of hell in a 10-cent town.

Not worth a zinc cent.

No better than a bogus hootenanny.

Nice as an icepick.

Tough as tripe.

Mean enough to steal cracklins from the grease.

Mean as gar broth.

More collared than greens. [*Said of an oft-arrested person*]

Even her dinner bell is off-key.

She'd rather climb a tree to tell a lie than to tell the truth on the ground.

I'm not saying he's a liar, but when it's time to feed his hogs, he has to get someone else to call 'em.

If she ever gets to heaven, she won't have nothing to do.

If I ordered a truckload of S.O.B's and they just sent him, I'd accept the shipment.

BIG, FAT

Heavy as a bucket of hog livers.

Big enough to choke a horse.

Big as a banker's barn.

Big as a boxcar.

Big as a bale of cotton.

Two ax handles wide.

Fat as a sausage salesman.

Plump as a partridge in pea time.

So fat you couldn't tell which wrinkle would open to talk.

Not enough dirt in Dallas to shovel him over.

Just a big ol' jelly bean.

She sleeps with her head in the kitchen and her feet
in the hall.

CERTAIN

I know it for a calcified fact.

Sure as sunrise.

Sure as a saved sinner.

Sure as a gun's iron.

Like it or lump it.

CHEAP

He's so cheap, he gets out of bed to turn over so he
won't wear out the sheets.

She's so cheap, she breathes through her nose to keep
from wearing out her false teeth.

She's so cheap, her pancakes have only one side.

CRAZY

As crazy as a locoed horse.

One taco short of a combination dinner.

He's got a few loose wingnuts.

She ain't wrapped too tight.

They left her out in the sun too long.

Cracky and notional.

More weevils than wheat.

All vines and no taters.

All wax and no wick.

DEAD

They took him out in a sack.

They sent his saddle home.

They brought him home sideways across the saddle.

He hung up his spurs.

He's all curled up like fried baloney.

Stone-cold dead in the morning.

Her dance card is empty. [*Also means "unpopular"*]

He passed on, but it wasn't anything serious.

I can hear the screws squeakin' in my coffin.

DIFFICULT

Like unbreaking an egg.

Like trying to take the shine off sausage.

Like trying to get a drink out of a fire hose.

That gun kicks as hard as it shoots.

DRUNK

Wall-eyed and whomper-jawed.
All lit up like the Fourth of July. [*Also means "excited"*]
Bitten by tarantula juice.
Drunk as Hoogan's goat.
Where'd your legs go?

DUMB

Not the sharpest crayon in the box.
Not the sharpest knife in the drawer.
Not a lot of grain in his silo.
Pig simple.
He couldn't figure out a seed catalog.
He couldn't mount a dashboard Jesus.
He ain't smart, he just acts that way.
He thinks he's read a book.
He don't know a brisket from a biscuit.
He don't know enough to salt meat.
She couldn't eat with the right end of the spoon.
She couldn't scratch her head with a fork.
She wouldn't recognize her own piglets.
She's running on a lean mixture.
A head like spoonbread.
Just as happy as if she had good sense.
No more sense than last year's bird nest.
No more sense than to keep out of the campfire.

Not enough sense to color her roots.

Nothing falls off an empty wagon.

His belt don't go all the way through the loops.

His bread ain't done.

If you bought him a book he'd chew off the covers.

EXCLAMATIONS

By the great horn spoon!

Give 'em what-for!

Pour the tea! [*and give me the details*]

Keep your jewels clear!

Wake up and bite the biscuits!

Well, don't that cock your pistol!

Rosin up the bow. ["*Get ready!*"]

I haven't laughed so hard since the mule drug Sister through the sticker patch.

I haven't laughed so hard since I wore three-cornered pants.

I had a fit and fell in it.

May the good Lord bless your skies.

EXPENSIVE

High as a hawk. [*Also means "drunk"*]

High as a tree. [*Also means "drunk"*]

Quail high.

That's not a lot of sugar for a dime.

FAST

She jumped on it like a duck on a junebug.

She jumped on it like a hen hawk on a settin' quail.

He jumped on it like a chicken on a Chee-to.

He runs so fast when he passes a piece of flint he strikes sparks with his bare toes.

Faster than you can say howdy-doo.

Faster than he could chew his tobacco twice.

Faster than a frog can lick flies.

GOOD

He'll do to take along.

She'll do to ride the river with.

She'll take up the slack.

He's about half preacher.

Straight as a shingle.

Better'n buttered grits.

Honest as buttermilk.

True as love and twice as likely.

She's cooked to a turn.

GENERAL ADVICE

A dog that brings home a bone leaves one, too.
    [*Beware of gossipers.*]

I've got a bone to pick with you. [*Also means "angry"*]

A hit dog always howls.

That's a hard dog to keep under the porch.

You got to kill a snake where you find it.

You better put on your big britches. [Be careful.]

That's like telling Noah about rain.

You ain't learning when you're talking.

A hog can't pass a good mud hole.

Crow don't taste like chicken.

Just grin and walk through the cannon smoke. [Hang on.]

Carry your own oil can.

Don't worry about the mule, just load the wagon.

Don't jump if you can't see bottom.

The more you run over a possum, the flatter it gets.

If you're destined to hang, you have no fear of
 drowning.

When the chips are down, be careful where you step.

Tight boots'll shrink all your other troubles.

Never look down at your boots. You can clean 'em
 off later.

Don't drink downstream from the herd.

Don't mess in the sandbox.

Common sense ain't.

Empty wagons rattle the loudest.

He can look farther and see less than any other person
 I know.

He's lathering up for a shave. [He's due for a
 comeuppance.]

A good horse is never a bad color.

Never thump a free melon.

HOT

Hot as a June bride in a featherbed.

Hot as a brisket.

Hot enough for biscuits.

IMMORAL, WILD

She's pullin' his taffy.

He's struttin' his okra.

She's done more spooning than Grandma's ladle.

Who's she playing horsey with now?

She'd wear pantaloons to a funeral.

She wears her clothes kind of sudden.

She lets her hair down and everything else, too.

They call her "Thermos," 'cause she'll keep anything
   warm.

She swallowed a watermelon seed. [*She's pregnant.*]

He's never been curried below the knees.
   [*He's uncivilized.*]

He's bobbin' for her apples.

He picked up a crooked stick. [*He made a bad marriage.*]

He left town when she named the baby.

He goes places a flyswatter wouldn't.

It's not how deep you fish, it's how you wiggle your worm.

Too close for country dancin'.

INSULTS

Grandma was slow, but she was old.

He's so slow his cooties run on ahead.

She'd make a damn fine piece of venison.

When she's dead, the worms won't eat her.

Her biscuits bake on the squat. [*She can't cook.*]

Here's a bandana—play outlaw. [*You're ugly.*]

Big hair, small brain.

The buffalo are gone, and his kind are still here.

We call her "Treasure," 'cause we wish she was buried somewhere.

Get me the flyswatter and I'll help you kill it. [*Said of a new hat or hairdo*]

If you need someone to push you in the creek, just let me know.

Your mama works offshore.

LAZY

He was born tired and never got rested up.

He follows the shade around the house.

She was born in the middle of the week looking both ways for Sunday.

She won't lift a finger to pick her own nose.

MISCELLANEOUS

Flatter than a road toad.

Gone as a bee-stung cat.

Out of there like a kerosened cat.

He keeps her on a short leash.

Stickier than a taffy pull.

Busy as a backhoe.

He could sweet-talk water from a well.

He's barking up the wrong tree.

Scary as a one-handed snake handler.

Chatty as an oyster.

Strong as truckstop coffee.

Beaten like a borrowed mule.

Quiet as a mouse spittin' on cotton.

As welcome as castor oil.

Your eyes are bigger than your stomach.

She stores up for the winter all year round.

She'd lend you her last soup bone.

She couldn't say boo to a goose.

So proper she won't fry a chicken breast.

Dark-thirty. [*Sunset, nighttime*]

Proud as a dog with two tails.

Strong enough to float a horseshoe. [*Said of coffee*]

He'd stand in the hedge and take up the gap.
    [*He's brave.*]

If it was raining soup, I'd be caught with a fork.

POOR

She don't earn enough to pay attention.

Mean as cat meat.

So poor they boiled the shadows of their starving hogs.

So poor he has to clean the chitlins himself.

Their shack was so small the dog wagged his tail up
    and down.

Nothing but bugs in the breadbox.

The railroad's his pillow, his blanket's the night.

She could pack her entire wardrobe in a matchbox.

PRETTY

You could throw her in a pond and skim off cute for a month.

You could put her in a croaker sack and she'd look good.

A neck-twister if ever there was one.

Reason enough to give up whiskey.

All dolled up like Dallas.

Tastier than a Moon Pie.

Stacked like a gambler's chips.

She plumb sunburned my eyes off.

She could make a preacher pitch his Bible in the creek.

No fly ever lit on her.

REMOTE, ISOLATED

They live four wagon greasings behind the post office.

I was raised so far back in the sticks that all us kids smelled like fresh-cut cordwood.

He lives so far out in the country, he has to walk into town to hunt.

So far out you can't hear the rooster crow.

SAD

She cried till her bones melted.

She fell apart like a flour-sack dress.

He's a one-man calamity convention.

Blue sick.

The blues arrived with a suitcase and a steamer trunk.

A face so long she could eat oats out of a churn.

Short

They picked her before she was ripe.

Short as a cigar stub.

Short as the day's take.

Shorter than shortening.

Born short and slapped down flat.

Sick

The wheels are falling off my wagon.

My sawdust is leaking.

He got the slats kicked out from under him.

He's heading through the gate and eyeing the river.

He's not pertin' up a-tall.

She's all right; she just can't do the laundry for a while.

She's circling the drain.

She's a permanent palleteer.

So sick he threw up his socks.

Small, Thin

No bigger than a cooked pea.

Not up to here on a stinkbug.

As big as a button.

Bump-boned.

Too thin to fry.

Thin as Bible paper.

Thin as a piggin' string.

Thin as a nun's smile.

Thin as the maid's sheets.

SMART, WISE

Wise as a treeful of owls.

Bright as a jarful of fireflies.

He's got bobcat logic.

He's all kinds of a man.

She don't wear no blinders.

She's heard the hoot owls hoot.

She reads so much, they treated her for bookworm.

It don't take him long to look at a horseshoe.

UGLY

She's so cross-eyed, when she cries the tears run down
her back.

He looks like a basted turkey.

He's so bald he carries his dandruff in his hip pocket.

He's so ugly he has to set a trap by his plate to catch
his appetite.

You look like you ran through the woods and the bears
got you.

You look like you've been hit in the face with a sack
full of nickels.

You look like something the dog wouldn't eat.

You can't tell from his face if he's laughing or crying.

He looks like the hindquarters of bad luck.

He looks like he was chewing tobacco and spit into the wind.

He could scare a mule away from his oats.

They turn his picture to the wall. [*Also means "disgraced"*]

A pie in the face would improve her looks something fierce.

Ugly as a stump full of spiders.

VAIN

He shaves the same face every morning. [*He puts on airs.*]

She leaves kiss marks all over her mirror.

She wouldn't go to a funeral unless she could be the corpse.

She walks like she's got oil wells in her backyard.

Too good to eat beans.

WEATHER

So cold I'm spitting hailstones.

So cold her behind matches her blue eyes.

Wet enough to bog a saddle blanket.

It rained a barbed-wire fence in two.

A chunk mover on all creeks.

You can sandblast your skillet clean by holding it over the key hole.

So windy I saw one hen lay the same egg five times.

So windy from the west the sun was three hours late
     going down.

When she fainted it took two buckets of dust to bring
     her around.

Bad water: too thin to plow, too thick to drink.

The mesquites ain't out. [*It's not spring yet; also, it's
     early.*]

So dry the fish have seed ticks.

So dry even a grass widow wouldn't take root.

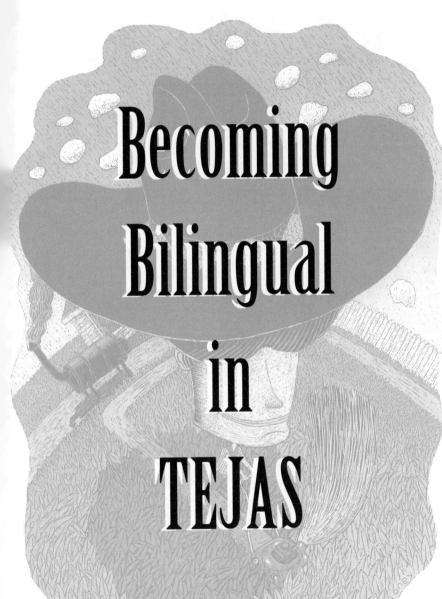

Becoming

Bilingual

in

TEJAS

odern Texans, native and newcomer alike, inevitably enjoy the pithiness and charm of country sayings—we take to them like hounds to ham bones. Few of us, however, other than tejanos (Hispanic Texans), appreciate a much older and even more engrained linguistic influence: Spanish. Perhaps our staunch monolinguism is a result of the nation's postwar superiority complex. The Texas Legislature has firmly rebuffed all attempts to make the state bilingual (even though Spanish preceded English as the region's common language—by a couple of hundred years, in fact—and Native American tongues preceded Spanish).

Most Texans, however, simply aren't regularly exposed to the language outside of Tex-Mex restaurant menus. For Spanish-speaking Texans, on the other hand, a passing knowledge of English is essential. The Texas State Data Center at Texas A&M predicts that by the year 2025, Hispanics will edge out Anglos as the biggest population group in the state. It's time to buy into bilingualism and learn *español*, y'all.

As for myself, however, I've been trying to learn Spanish for more than a decade—since my children were babies—and all I've really mastered is what *not* to say. My first intensive exposure to the language occurred when a wonderful woman named Beatriz started caring for my kids. Now a U.S. citizen, she was then freshly arrived from San Luís Potosí, and her English was nonexistent. The first time I called Beatriz's house and she answered

the phone, "Bueno," I thought I had the wrong number—I could have sworn her last name was Martinez.
"Bueno" in that context, however, just means "hello."
(It's rather like saying "Well?" to an English speaker to
urge her to continue.)

My first few attempts at conversing with Beatriz ran
along the lines of "Oh, what coffee!" and "I am return-
ing yesterday" and "How fat the dust!" Although my
vocabulary grew, it remained largely child-related for a
long time and of limited use in conversations with other
adults. ("The nipples are dirty. Is there a fever in your
diapers?") Eventually, however, I could exchange basic
pleasantries, but only in the present tense. Spanish verbs
became my personal Alamo.

Still, as Lyle Lovett put it, "What are you if you don't
try?" Remember, better (trans)late now than never; a
rolling stone gathers no *más*; no guts, no *gloría*. Below is
a quickie overview of what may someday be Texas' offi-
cial language once again. It's far from complete—think of
it as the grated cheese, not the whole enchilada—but it
may whet your appetite for more.

First of all, learning the language begins with playing
musical vowels. "A" is never flat but always soft, as in
"paw." "E" sounds more like "eh." "I" sounds like a long
"E"—the word *mi* means "me," and is pronounced exactly the same way. The letter "O," *grácias a Dios*, is usually
sounded like a long O (or the short "oh") in English. "U"
is kind of a crooned "ooh" sound, as in "mood" or "boom."

Thus, to English speakers, the word *amable* ("likable") appears to rhyme with "wobble," but in fact it's "ah-MAHB-leh," while *estupido* is "ess-STOOP-pee-dough."

Consonants cause trouble, too. "H" is usually silent, as in the English word "herb." The familiar greeting "Hola!" for example, is pronounced "OWE-lah." So what *does* sound like an "H"? "J," of course. (Isn't this fun?) In Mexican comic books—which I have discovered are excellent learning aids, by the way—the villains always laugh with a *"Je, je, je."*

Spanish even has four *extra* consonants, just to keep things interesting. "Ch" is its own letter. "Ñ"—it has to have that little squiggle on top of it—has a "nyah" sound, like the common playground taunt. The word *cañón*, for example, may look like "cannon" to us, but it's pronounced "con-YOAN" and is the cognate for "canyon."

Two consonants in Spanish are actually made up of double letters: "rr"—which, as it suggests by its very appearance, is double-trilled, a linguistic flourish (absent in American English) that requires rapid tongue work. Thus, *burro*—which rhymes with "thorough" in English—becomes "BOOR-row." There's no "L" sound in the letter "ll." Instead, it's pronounced like our consonant "Y." Consider the word "tortilla"—common enough nationwide that it is rarely mispronounced even by confirmed Yankees.

Speaking of Yankees, the Spanish word *"Yanquis"* looks and sounds like it might be interchangeable with that Southern epithet. But "Yanquis" is an example of what linguists like to call "false friends"—words that suggest one thing but mean another. To Texans and Southerners, for example, a Yankee is a Northerner, someone who hails from north of the Mason-Dixon line. To Mexicans and other Spanish speakers, however, *Yanquis* are Americans, period—a.k.a. *norteamericanos*. The slang term *"gringo"* means roughly the same thing, but is considered derogatory.

Lots of common words in Spanish look like English words, but don't assume they mean the same thing. *Café*, for example, is not a coffee shop but "coffee," period. *Colorado* means not the polygonal state northwest of us but "colored," specifically colored red (the Colorado River was named for the hue of its mud); *chile colorado* is the Mexican equivalent of our chili.

If you eat bad chili at a diner, you may end up *intoxicado*—which means poisoned, not drunk; the latter is *borracho*, and could lead to a *crudo*—a hangover. ("Beer," by the way, is *cerveza* in Spanish, and many a Tex-Mex joint posts signs stating, "No shirt, no shoes, no *cerveza*.") If you're south of the border on vacation, you're a tourist but not a *turista*—that Hispanicizing of our word means, basically, "the trots," or "Montezuma's revenge"—a common tourist's complaint.

Excusado isn't "excuse" or "excused"; it's colloquial for "toilet," which is certainly a good excuse if you need one. Or, let's say a woman misuses the word *excusado*, and then wants to say she is embarrassed. If she dredges up the word *embarazada*, she will be doubly embarrassed—it means "pregnant" in Mexican idiom. (This is not much odder than the English euphemism "expecting.")

The word *embarazada* brings up another important rule in Spanish. Unlike English, in which words apply democratically—as-is—to male and female alike, Spanish nouns and adjectives are either masculine (in which case they generally end in "-o") or feminine (typically ending in "-a")

Of course there are exceptions, but don't worry your pretty little *cabeza* about that right now. Thus, *embarazada* must end in an "-a"; a man stating he is *embarazado* would invite speculation as to both his sexual orientation and his mental health. Even "the" gets tailored to the gender of the word or person involved; *el* is masculine singular, *los* plural; *la* is feminine singular, *las* plural.

Nouns and adjectives also have to match up in number as well as gender: *los norteamericanos feos*, the ugly Americans; *la lengua extraña*, the strange language. Note, too, that in Spanish, adjectives generally follow the nouns they modify, which is the opposite of English. That can make for an experience frustrating.

Because of the preponderance of Spanish words ending in "o", and because a few of those are universally familiar to Americans— say, *loco* and *taco*—adventurous conversationalists may attempt to stick an "o" on the end of an English word and hope the result makes sense. Sometimes, it will: *Fino* is "fine," and *rápido* means "fast."

But don't try it in the case of, say, the word "cool." The result is *culo*, which refers to a certain part of the, er, fundament and is a highly objectionable profanity.

Another word whose linguistic scrambling commonly evokes amusement is *huevos*, which literally means "eggs" but is slang for "testicles." To be on the safe side, never ask the waiter at your favorite Mexican restaurant, "*¿Tiene huevos?*" ("Do you have eggs?") Better stick with "*huevos rancheros, por favor.*"

And speaking of *hombres*, kids never call their daddy "papa"—that means potato. They use, among other terms, "*papá*"—with an accent on the second syllable. And here's another example of how "false friends" can trip you up: If you ask for potatoes to go with those *huevos rancheros,* make sure the word you use is plural and feminine—*las papas*—not singular and masculine—*El Papa.* That would be ordering a side dish of the Pope—a mistake, no matter how divine the food may be.

Note all the accents sprinkled around like pepper. They help you recognize which syllable to emphasize in a particular word that doesn't follow standard Spanish style. It's hard enough to remember them, but if you really want to feel stupid, try writing the upside-down question mark that precedes every interrogative in Spanish. And then there are Spanish verbs, which require more time and trouble than tamales. One of the trickiest for English speakers is "is."

In Spanish, there are five verbs for "to be." The most common forms are *ser* and *estar*. *Ser* conveys permanence, while *estar* means physical location and impermanence. The difference can be crucial: "*Ella es buena,*" using a form of *ser*, for example, means "She is nice"—a permanent state—while "*Ella está buena,*" using a form of *estar*, puts a sexual connotation to "She's good."

Similarly, "*El está enfermo,*" means "He is ill," while "*El es enfermo*" means "He's a sicko." In addition, the verb *tener*, which usually means "to have," can mean "to be" when it's combined with certain nouns. "*Tengo hambre,*" for example, means "I'm hungry," but literally states "I have hunger."

Again, the idiom is important: "*Tengo calor,*" for example, refers to temperature—"I'm hot"—but "*Soy caliente*" translates as "I'm a hot babe," and "*Estoy caliente*" asserts that "I am in heat."

Finally, one form of *haber*—*hay*—can mean "there is," while *hacer*—meaning to do or make—means "is" for weather purposes: "*Hace frío*" is "it's cold." Whereas English offers only a clunky, one-size-fits-all version of "to be," the multiple meanings of the Spanish equivalents help give the language great subtlety—as do the two forms of the pronoun "you."

In English, "you" is a general-purpose word, applicable to anyone from toddlers to total strangers. But in Spanish there are two you's: One, *usted*, is polite and formal; the other, *tu*, is familiar and informal. Many people use *tu* for young children, whether they know them or not, but address an adult stranger as *usted*. A couple going out on a blind date, for example, would start off using *usted*, in the hopes of being *tu* by evening's end. This apparently minor shift in formality can have a major impact on meaning.

One consolation, however, is that, for native Spanish speakers, learning English is surely worse. The verb "take," for example, changes its meaning depending on whether you take on, take off, take in, take out, take up, take down, take to, take back, take around, take after, take part, or take over.

Then there are idioms that, if translated literally, are idiotic: "take a powder," say, or "that takes the cake." Wannabe English-speakers must simply take their time, take stock, and take heart from the immortal words of Doris *Día: Que será, será.*

Following is a list of sentences, with approximate phonetic pronunciation, to help even the most monolingual of Texans venture into Spanish territory. Bolstered with a few basic phrases such as *muchas grácias* (thank you very much) and *lo siento* (I'm sorry—literally, "I feel it"), they can help you navigate tricky international waters while offering pertinent applications to modern Lone Star life.

1. *Perdone mi mal español, pero no soy tan inteligente como parezco.* (Pehr-DOUGH-kneh me mall ess-PAHN-yole, PAIR-oh know soi tahn inn-telly-HINT-teh CO-moe par-REZ-coe.) Pardon my bad Spanish, but I am not as smart as I look.

2. *El baño está ocupado. Creo que voy a reventar.* (Ell BAHN-yoe ess-TAH awk-coo-POD-oh. CREH-oh kay voy ah REV-inn-tar.) The bathroom is occupied. I think I'm going to explode.

3. *¿Cuanto cuesta esta bonita rana morada de cerámica? Creo que a mi suegra le va a encantar!* (KWAN-toe QUEST-ah ESS-tah bo-NEE-tah RAH-nah MORE-odd-ah deh sair-RAHM-eke-uh? CREH-oh keh ah me SWAY-grah leh vah ah inn-CAHN-tar.) How much is this lovely purple plaster frog? My mother-in-law will love it!

4. *Buenos días, oficial. ¿De que lado de la frontera estoy?* (BWEH-knows DEE-ahs, owe-fee-see-all. Deh keh LAH-dough deh lah frahn-TAIR-uh ess-TOY?) Good morning, officer. What side of the border am I on?

5. *Ya me canse de verte trabajar tanto. Voy a tomar una siesta.* (Yah meh CAHN-seh deh VAIR-teh TRAWB-ah-har TAHN-toe. Voy ah toe-mar ooh-nah see-ESS-tah.) I am tired of watching you work so hard. I'm going to take a nap.

6. *¿Tiene aspirinas? El tequila me da dolor de cabeza.* (Tee-INN-eh ass-purr-REEN-ahs? El teh-KEEL-ah meh dah doe-lore deh cah-BEH-sah.) Do you have any aspirin? Tequila gives me a headache.

7. *Por favor, llame una ambulancia. Esta salsa ya me derritio la lengua.* (Pore fah-vore, yah-meh ooh-nah ahm-boo-LAHNTS-see-ah. Ess-tah sahl-sah yah meh dare-

REET-tee-oh lah LING-gwah.) Please call an ambulance. This hot sauce has melted my tongue.

8. *Los tacos estuvieron buenisimos, pero no traigo dinero para pagarlos. Sin embargo, puedo correr rápido.* (Lows TOCK-ohs ess-TOO-vee-air-roan BWEH-knee-see-mose, PEHR-oh no treh-ego din-AIR-oh par-ah pah-GAR-lows. Seen em-BAR-go, PWEH-do core-air RAH-pee-dough.) The tacos were delicious, but I don't have the money to pay for them. However, I can run very fast.

9. *¡Oye, que feo estas! Te puedo recomendar a un cirujano plastico.* (OY-ay, keh FEH-oh ess-tahs. Teh PWEH-

dough wreck-COMB-men-dar ah oon seer-ooh-hahn-know PLAHS-tee-coe.) How ugly you are! I can recommend a plastic surgeon.

10. ¿Donde están las pinsitas? Me sente en una nopalera y me llene las "pompas" de espinas. (DAWN-deh ess-TAHN lahs peen-SEAT-tahs? Meh SEN-teh inn ooh-nah know-pall-AIR-rah ee meh YEH-ney lahs POMP-ahs deh ess-PEEN-ahs.) Where are the tweezers? I sat on a cactus, and there are many spines in my butt.

Pass the Salsa

In a nutshell, here's the substance of true Texas food: It's often bad for the bod, but good for the soul. The state's time-honored culinary rule might be "If from the first you want to succeed, fry, fry again." Historically, the state's cuisine has focused on beef—the foodstuff most likely to be cheap and available.

The meat of range-fed cattle was also likely to be gristly and tough, so cow-camp cooks and ranch wives soon learned to fry the living daylights out of it—the nineteenth-century equivalent of meat tenderizing.

Eventually, a staple of the region became what is possibly the most beloved single item of Texas fare, the chicken-fried steak—a slab of beef double-dipped in egg and flour, then fried and topped with cream gravy—a heart-stoppingly fine plate of grub.

Barbecue—meat roasted over an open fire pit—is and was equally adored and consumed in massive quantities. Novelist-historian George Sessions Perry once wrote, "In Texas, we barbecue anything that will hold still."

Of course, back in the good ol' days, most diners headed out after such a major midday repast to dig postholes, ride fence, break horses, hand-wring laundry, or perform one of hundreds of other laborious tasks, so they had no problem working off the thousands of calories in such a mega-meal.

Unfortunately, while today's Texans are more likely to sit in an office chair all day, they have retained their taste for the heavy, cholesterol-ridden meals of their ancestors, and some 30 percent of us qualify as medically obese. Will we ever forsake our fondness for beef and grease? Fat chance. The mere thought hits us right in the brisket.

Second only to beef as a Texas favorite is Mexican food or, as it is generally referred to, Tex-Mex, since the dishes are not authentically Mexican or specifically Texan but a mixture of the two. In addition to tacos, enchiladas, and other items now renowned throughout the U.S., Tex-Mex relies heavily on two staples: the tortilla and the chile pepper.

The tortilla is essentially Mexican cornbread—an unleavened round of flatbread served either freshly griddle-cooked or crisply fried into taco shells or tostadas, a.k.a. tortilla chips. Texans can claim not a kernel of credit for the corn tortilla, a New World delicacy created deep within Mexico. Instead, they tend to go against the grain and opt for a different variety: the flour tortilla, whose popularity indeed has flowered in the last decade or two. This hybrid resulted from the American love of white bread and the convenience of the edible wrapping.

The flour tortilla is used to enfold any number of yummy stuffings, from scrambled eggs and *chorizo* (spicy sausage) to pinto beans and cheese. This make-it-yourself meal-on-the-run is called a soft taco, because the tortilla remains unfried, except in the morning when it is hawked as a breakfast taco. In the Rio Grande Valley, breakfast tacos are called *mariachis*, perhaps because they serenade your stomach.

As essential to Tex-Mex as the tortilla is the chile, a hot pepper that imparts to Tex-Mex its distinctive flair— or perhaps "flare" is the right word, because chiles range from mildly tangy to downright incendiary. The plainest, most vegetable-like variety is the poblano chile, which resembles an elongated (but often paler) bell pepper. Egg-battered and filled with meat or cheese, it stars in the popular dish called the *chile relleno* ("stuffed chile").

Most common among chiles is the jalapeño, a dark green pepper about the size of a man's thumb. The Texified pronunciation is, roughly, "hall-a-PAIN-yo"—with the emphasis on "pain." While novice eaters may feel they have accidentally chowed down on cleverly disguised industrial solvent, jalapeños are, in fact, only medium-hot compared to the *habanero*—a puny little pepper that makes up in punch what it lacks in size. Taking even the tiniest nibble of habanero is inviting a near-death experience. Your entire life will pass in front of your eyes—well, maybe it's just a flood of tears distorting your vision—and your taste buds and nerve endings from lip to lap immediately mutiny.

So why would anyone have a burning desire to eat habaneros at all? Aside from the fact that chiles are native to the region, and thus a ready food source, there are two basic theories. According to one, capsaicin—the chemical irritant that is the active ingredient in hot peppers—makes you break out in a sweat and thus cools you down. The other theory contends that this same heat-streaking-missile part of the pepper becomes almost addictive to regular eaters, who gradually build up an immunity of sorts but continue to crave the burn.

At any rate, proceed cautiously around peppers, particularly the table salsa that is a condiment in every Tex-Mex cafe—as ubiquitous and *importante* as salt. Salsa—

also called "picante sauce," from the Spanish word *picante* meaning "biting"—can be either green or red; the former is usually milder, the latter lavalike. But odds are you'll eventually come to lava the taste.

Both chiles and beef are de rigueur in chili. Note the spelling difference: "chili" with an "i," meaning the stew-like main dish, is an Anglicization of long standing; "chile" with an "e" is the vegetable. (Neither, however, is ever "chilly," in spelling, temperature, or level of spice.) The word "chili" is actually a corruption of the Mexican term *chile con carne,* meaning "chiles with meat." The dish is a contribution of nameless cooks in Old San Antonio; as long as the 1850s, enterprising señoras set up food stands in that city's plaza and dished up bowls of the homemade stew to ravenous *vaqueros* and other visitors.

Chili, like chiles, can be spicy or mild. And the chili cookoff, a celebratory event built up around its preparation, has become a standard arena of modern Texas machismo. Cooks, both male and female, vie at contests all over the state to make the hottest chili—or the reddest, or the thickest, or the weirdest.

Willis residents Cynthia Hudson and Robert Zirl, for instance, conjure up a new variety every year for his hospital's annual chilifest. The results have been variously labeled "Bob's Look What the Cat Dragged In Chili," which boasted the ever-popular secret ingredient (I don't know what it was, but participants surely realized he's a pathologist); "Bob's Rheal Good Chili," made with the meat of the rhea, a cousin of the ostrich; and (my favorite) "Bob's Navy Chili—Don't Ask, Don't Tell."

Purists contend that a true "bowl of red" has no tomatoes and that chili should derive its color solely from peppers and spices. Lots of Texans throw in some tomatoes anyway, but most studiously avoid the most serious Texas chili no-no: adding beans. Native cooks are more likely to add pinto pony than pinto beans. Anyone who commits this faux pas clearly doesn't know beans about the Texas state dish.

At this point, readers who are vegetarians—if they have made it this far—have blanched the color of cream gravy. Never fear. For the state's ever-growing contingent of non-meat eaters, there is plenty of indigenous produce that allows you to eat healthily and fat-free.

Pecos cantaloupe, for instance, is the apotheosis of melonhood; its ambrosial flavor, fragrance, and feel result from the sunny climate and alkaline soil surrounding the town of Pecos. Alas, the melon is only available from mid- to late summer; the rest of the year, its absence makes Texans—well, melon-choly.

Other in-season treats include Poteet strawberries—a seedy little specialty grown in and around the small town south of San Antonio for which they're named (where the water tower is painted to resemble the vaunted berry)—and, from the fertile fields of the lower Rio Grande Valley, Rio Red grapefruit, which is another ruddy good fruit and one that gives new meaning to the phrase "sweet and sour." There's also Texmati rice (a customized hybrid of the Basmati variety), tasty Texas 1015 onions (which are just as peachy as Georgia's famous Vidalias), and dozens more incredible edibles.

In the beverage category, Texans have long excelled at brewing, thanks to broods of Germans who immigrated to Texas in the nineteenth century. Texans have long been partial to Lone Star beer—with a name like that, how could they not be?—but that brand is not the lone star among Texas beer choices. Although Pearl is a gem, too, many Texans long ago took a shine to Shiner, a long-independent brewery that manufactures its various labels of beer in the town of the same name.

From a different cultural heritage comes Texas' other favorite alcoholic drink—tequila, distilled in Mexico from a type of native plant called the *agave*. The agave is somewhat similar to another genus, the yucca, and its potent liquor provokes many a yuck or chuckle, depending on the imbiber.

Texans generally quaff tequila in the form of the margarita—a mixed or frozen concoction that also includes lime juice and Triple Sec, served in a glass rimmed with salt. The exact origins of the margarita are unclear—big

surprise there—but Texans naturally favor the tale that credits its creation to an El Paso bartender in 1942. (Odds are, though, that the story is just a hangover from past folklore.)

Other than the margarita, tequila is most generally consumed in shots but, once again, enhanced with salt and lime and a carefully prescribed ritual. The drinker holds a wedge of lime between his thumb and forefinger, and then licks the web between those two digits—the better to secure the salt he sprinkles there next. Then he licks off the salt, downs a straight shot of tequila, and no one has to tell him what to do with the lime. It's an intoxicating experience—give it a shot some time.

Unlike beer, all the great tequilas are manufactured in Mexico. Texas, however, has plenty of other bragworthy products that have made a name for themselves nationwide while remaining a favorite among Texas consumers. Read on for a list of eight great brands that have left their mark on Texas.

Imperial Sugar. The Imperial Sugar Company gave rise to the Houston exurb of Sugar Land and is one of Texas' oldest continuously operating manufacturing plants. Shortly after the Civil War, a local plantation owner discovered that the region's soil suited sugar cane and sugar beet production, and that affinity helped sweeten the odds for Imperial's success. Many a young Texan learned to cook from Imperial Sugar's "My First Cookbook," and promotional publications aimed at adult cooks advocated adding sugar to the likes of gumbo and beans.

Some sugar production takes place on nearby state prison farms, and an attempted breakout from one of them became a central plot device in Steven Spielberg's first feature film, *The Sugarland Express* (1974).

Gebhardt Chili. This venerable San Antonio-based company, which grew famous around the turn of the century for convenience foods targeted at shortcut-loving Anglo cooks. Its many giveaway recipe pamphlets helped promote the creation of Tex-Mex by toning down spicy Mexican foods; its recipes also advised cooks to perk up such items as fruit salad or deviled eggs with chili powder. Today, its canned chili is a staple for bachelors (and bachelorettes) statewide.

Pace Picante. Yet another San Antonio product, Pace was founded in 1947, which makes it the pacesetter as far as mass-produced salsas are concerned. Its original formula soon diverged into mild, medium, hot, and extra-hot incarnations, for leather-tongued Texans and less masochistic Mexican-food fans (who, in terms of spiciness, had to learn to pace themselves).

In 1994, the company was acquired by the New Jersey company that also owns the Campbell's Soup brand. The move temporarily chilled the hot-sauce company's loyalists, but ultimately, in terms of damage, the sale did zip to its zippy products' popularity.

Fritos. San Antonian Elmer Doolin popularized the salty corn chip that is now a cornerstone of the giant snack-food company Frito-Lay, which is headquartered in Dallas. According to company lore, Doolin paid $100 in 1932 to an anonymous Hispanic gentleman for the recipe. Its subsequent success must have put a chip on the seller's shoulder.

Note that Fritos can be combined with Gebhardt's chili to produce a puredee-Texan foodstuff, Frito pie, that is served everywhere from greasy spoons to school cafeterias. The dish involves simply pouring chili over Fritos, then sprinkling grated cheese and chopped onions on top. Vintage Texas cookbooks recommend allotting one five-cent bag of Fritos per person and pouring the chili directly into the bag. Regardless of how you make it, though, Frito pie is guaranteed to chip away at your hunger pains.

Ste. Genevieve. Though not as vintage an industry as brewing, winemaking began making grape strides in Texas agriculture in the late '70s, when far-sighted agriculturists discovered that much of Texas' soil and climate was just fine for grapevines. Ste. Genevieve owes its success to an unusual Franco-Texan alliance, which paired French expertise with West Texas vineyards. Texans eagerly embraced this newest of native yields and, for many resident oenophiles today, life is a cabernet.

Old El Paso. Canny cannery has long purveyed green chiles, tomatoes, and ready-to-eat Mexican foods from the headquarters in its titular city, where the fertile Rio Grande Valley and the chile fields of neighboring New Mexico provide ample resources. The company evokes not just Texas but the entire Southwest with its label, which erroneously depicts a saguaro cactus. That's the one that resembles a goalpost or a traffic policeman; it is actually native only to Old Mexico, New Mexico, and Arizona. Customers are so accustomed to the cactus label, however, that the company has stuck with it despite protests from prickly purists.

Dr Pepper. Arguably Texas' most famous product, Dr Pepper was the creation of a Waco pharmacist named Charles Alderton. His experiments with spice, fruit flavorings, and carbonation fizzled until one fateful day in 1885 when he hit the right combo and began offering the happy result to local soda-fountain patrons, who dubbed it a "Waco."

Gambling on going national, Alderton rechristened his beverage "Dr Pepper"—the "Dr" because it appeared to lend a medical endorsement, and "Pepper" perhaps for a former employer—or perhaps because the drink itself was a pepper-upper.

Sales of Dr Pepper, at first strictly Southern, eventually soared; in 1988, the company merged with another soft-drink biggie, 7Up, and seven years later the international beverage company Cadbury Schweppes bought both labels for a staggering $1.7 billion. Wouldn't you like to own a piece of Dr Pepper, too?

Pangburn's. The marketing of the Fort Worth-based chocolate candies is chockfull of Texas ties. The company's sampler assortment of candies was long dubbed the Roundup, and the artwork on the boxes featured cowboy-hatted lasses, borders of curving lassos, and other western motifs. Today, Pangburn's continues to butter up Texans and cream the local competition with other tips of the hat to Texas pride—such as its 1998 series of candy tins featuring bluebonnets and other wildflower motifs.

From the Ink Wells of the Lone Star State

For a long time, Texans were known to be more comfortable with oil wells than ink wells, with cattle pens rather than ink pens. For well over a century, most of the writing about Texas boiled down to snippy travelogues, syrupy poetry, and pioneer memoirs.

After an 1854 visit to Texas, for example, New Yorker Frederick Law Olmsted wrote *A Journey Through Texas, or, A Saddle-trip Through the Southwestern Frontier,* in which he described various Texans and their lives in "an actual wilderness" as "stupid," "uninstructed," "lazy," "sour," or "aggravating"—and his was one of the kinder reports.

Fortunately, however, after World War II, the state's burgeoning sophistication changed all that. The grand-pappy of Texas literature was certainly J. Frank Dobie, whose entertaining (if greatly overlapping) books covered many Texas icons and legends, such as longhorns, buried treasure, and cowboy life. A major Dobie cohort was historian Walter Prescott Webb, whose academic takes on Texas history included labeling the Mexican "inferior to the Comanche and wholly unequal to the Texan."

Later, acclaimed writer Katherine Anne Porter, raised in tiny Indian Creek, produced the novel *Ship of Fools* (1962) and the Pulitzer-winning *Collected Stories* (1966). Today, the best-known Texas litterateur by far is Larry McMurtry, who made his name with *In a Narrow Grave* (1961), a collection of essays dissing the state he had left. Ironically, the traditional Texanness he then despised later powered his many historical novels, particularly *Lonesome Dove*.

McMurtry's success further opened the door for Texas writers; today, many ply their trade in Texas, including best-selling novelists like romance queen Sandra Brown of Dallas and Edgar Award-winning mystery maven Mary Willis Walker of Austin.

Of course, many non-Texans, too, felt compelled to write about such a mythic and macho state. Naturally, most of these books went over poorly with the native populace. In 1925, for example, Virginia-born Dorothy Scarborough published *The Wind*, a tale of a genteel Southern girl and her travails in cruel West Texas; it was strictly of the "I can't pay the rent!"/"You must pay the rent!" school.

Wisely, Scarborough published her drivel anonymously, because it enraged Texans. So did Edna Ferber's *Giant* (1952), with its brash, crude characters and its skewering of Anglo-Texan relations. (Texans loved the softer film version, though—could it have been the presence of hunky Rock Hudson, sultry James Dean, and stunning Elizabeth Taylor?)

Following is a chronological list of 10 classic Texas books—not the ultimate list, by any means, but merely a sampling of the Lone Star State's varied, and very good, writings. If any pique your interest, dig deeper; Texas writers have produced 10 tomes as much.

Interwoven: A Pioneer Chronicle, Sallie Reynolds Matthews (1936). A tale of two West Texas ranching clans whose lives repeatedly intertwined, this memoir is a delightful compendium of customs and crises in pioneer days.

Hold Autumn in Your Hand, George Sessions Perry (1941). Underrated Rockdale native penned possibly the best-ever agrarian novel, which spans a year in the life of a tenant farmer. It became the movie *The Southerner*, starring Texas boy Zachary Scott.

Old Yeller, Fred Gipson (1956). Arguably the best dog novel ever written, it's the tale of a 14-year-old pioneer left in charge of his Hill Country home while his father is away. A classic for all ages. The Disney movie version debuted in Mason, Gipson's hometown.

Love Is a Wild Assault, Elithe Hamilton Kirkland (1959). Although a bit dated, perhaps, to modern ears, this romance still holds up; the love story is based on the practically cinematic life of Harriet Potter Ames, who indulged in a scandalous affair with Robert Potter, one-time Secretary of the Texas Navy.

A Woman of the People, Benjamin Capps (1966). Undersung writer produced characters so good you miss them long after the last page. This novel relates the life of a white child captured by Comanches and later

revered as a wise woman. Based loosely on the life of
Cynthia Ann Parker, whose son Quanah Parker later
became the tribe's last chief.

Blessed McGill, Edwin Shrake (1968). The title character
is, putatively, the first North American to be canonized
by the Catholic Church—a statement that, while true,
in a way misrepresents the novel itself, which is an
engrossing, finely written western romp. Shrake is also
famed for his sports writing.

The Wolf and the Buffalo, Elmer Kelton (1980). This set-
tle-in-and-read narrative follows the fortunes and misfor-
tunes of a buffalo soldier (the nickname for a black cav-
alryman) and a Comanche warrior. San Angelan Kelton
wrote the novel at his publisher's request to satisfy a
growing market for minority-oriented novels, and the
result—written by an Anglo—is remarkable for, among
other things, its complete lack of self-consciousness.
Gideon and Gray Wolf are as empathetic and likable as
humans can be.

Lonesome Dove, Larry McMurtry (1986). In Texas, it is
practically illegal to compile a list of great Texas books
and not include this Pulitzer prize-winning tome. The
motley crew of Texans in this novel take far too long to
depart the titular town and set out on a trail drive, but
once they do, you'd better plan on calling in sick for the

next week or so. The TV miniseries, written by Austinite Bill Wittliff, is equally fine.

All the Pretty Horses, Cormac McCarthy (1992). A National Book Award winner, this intense western by an El Paso recluse is set in 1949 and follows the fortunes of two teenage boys who escape their hardscrabble Texas ranch life and flee to Mexico. A gore-and-guts, testosterone-ridden adventure.

The Liars' Club, Mary Karr (1995). This huge best-seller, a compelling memoir of a young girl's upbringing in an ugly, stinky, coastal refinery town, is eloquent, raw, and unforgettable.

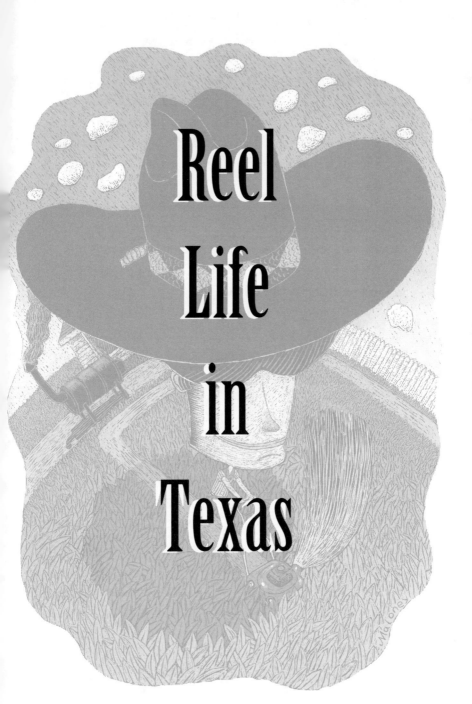

Reel

Life

in

Texas

L ike everything else in Texas' past, moviemaking in and about Texas was long western-themed. Many a grainy "oater" graced the silver screen (and later, the small one), and star turns as white-hatted heroes made John Wayne, Roy Rogers, Tom Mix, and many other cowboy actors honorary Texans in the eyes of their Lone Star audiences.

Westerns dominated Texas moviedom for some 40 years. But, ironically, the first award-winning film made in the state wasn't a western but a paean to military aviation; *Wings*, filmed in San Antonio, won the first-ever best-picture Academy Award in 1929.

Today, now that westerns as a genre have ridden into the sunset, Texas-made movies range from action thrillers (*RoboCop 2*) and war dramas (*Courage Under Fire*), to period pieces (*Places in the Heart*) and romantic comedies (*Home Fries*). Texas movies have also covered oil (*Boom Town, Written on the Wind*), small towns (*Hope Floats, 1918*), horror flicks (*Piranha, The Swarm*), and documentary subjects (*A Well-Spent Life, The Thin Blue Line*).

Many directors have visited the state to make genuinely Texan movies—made here, set here—including the venerated John Ford (*Two Rode Together*), the late French artist Louis Malle (*Alamo Bay*), and Australia's Bruce Beresford (*Tender Mercies*). Scores of productions have proved just the ticket for Texas audiences, who never tire of their state's appeal (nor, apparently, do out-of-staters). Following, for both old-timers and newcomers, is a carefully screened—well, sort-of-screened list of 15 fun Texas flicks, for all but seen-'em-all cinema buffs.

Giant (1956). Director George Stevens won the Academy Award for this big ol' Texas-size epic about cultural and generational conflicts. There was no lone star here: Rock Hudson shines as rancher Bick Benedict; James Dean, in his last film, is effective as upstart oilman Jett Rink; Elizabeth Taylor, too, comes off well as a Yankee transplant. A giant in the Texas film pantheon.

The Alamo (1960). Overlong, flawed, and tremblingly romantic, but it's still the best Alamo movie, with a bang-up final battle scene. And who else but the Duke (a.k.a. John Wayne) should play Davy Crockett, the king of the Alamo heroes? Don't expect realism: Susannah Dickinson leaves the mission in makeup and high heels.

Two Rode Together (1961). Unlike its sister film *The Searchers*, which was also directed by John Ford (and is even better), this western was made in Texas at Alamo Village, a production set in Brackettville run by former mayor Happy Shahan. Like *The Searchers*, however, it involves the rescue of Indian captives. James Stewart plays the marshal and Richard Widmark, a cavalry officer.

Hud (1963). Powerful father-and-son, past-and-present saga stars Paul Newman in a surprisingly mean turn.

Melvyn Douglas and Patricia Neal also star in this poignant ranching story. Shocking scene near the end will stay with you a long time.

Bonnie and Clyde (1967). Directed by Arthur Penn and written by UT film school graduate Robert Benton (later a prominent director himself), this tale of outlaw lovers in 1930s Texas and Louisiana made cinematic history with its graphic, stylized murder scenes.

Urban Cowboy (1980). Based on a story by writer Aaron Latham, a native of Spur, this movie with its apparently oxymoronic title presents a likable portrait of modern Texans' beliefs and myths. This film features the famous mechanical bull and also perfectly captures the often-mechanical bullying that characterizes some Texas menfolk.

Waltz Across Texas (1982). Lightweight romantic comedy fueled by the enduring conflict of independent oilman vs. corporate oil pigs. Not a gusher of tears or laughter, but enjoyable nonetheless. The heroine is played by a very young Anne Archer.

Songwriter (1984). A trio of native Texans—Willie Nelson, Kris Kristofferson, and Rip Torn—made movie music together in this white-hats-vs.-black-hats romp. It's a ditty, not an anthem, but kind of catchy nonetheless.

The Trip to Bountiful (1985). Geraldine Page won the best-actress Oscar for her portrayal of an elderly woman who wants to visit her little Texas hometown one last time. The lovely screenplay is by Wharton native Horton Foote, who won Oscars for two earlier efforts—his adaptation of Harper Lee's *To Kill a Mockingbird* and his original script for *Tender Mercies*. Not for action buffs, but poignant and pleasing.

Dazed and Confused (1993). Directed by Austin's Richard Linklater, this wry retrospective of a 1976 Texas high school graduating class is crammed with instantly identifiable times and types. It also launched the acting career of UT graduate Matthew McConaughey, who was born in Uvalde and grew up in Longview.

True Stories (1986). David Byrne, formerly the frontman for the Talking Heads, debuted as a director with this self-conscious, off-the-wall look at small-town-Texas sense and sensibilities. Stellar moments include a fundamentalist preacher assuring his congregation that "Texas is still paying for John Kennedy's death, my friends." As film scholar Leonard Maltin summed it up: "Is there anything easier to satirize than eccentric Lone Star crazies?"

Desperado (1995). Austin director Robert Rodriguez redid his homemade, shoestring thriller, *El Mariachi*, into this big-budget Antonio Banderas vehicle, which also made the sexy Salma Hayek a star. An heir to the *Bonnie and Clyde* viva-violence school, it was filmed along the Texas-Mexico border with a seductive Latin-rock score.

Lone Star (1996). Audience-friendly director John Sayles combines anti-Hispanic prejudice, a bad-boy sheriff, and small-town secrecy into this indie winner. Stars include Texans Matthew McConanghey and Kris Kristofferson. Worth watching for the final line alone.

Hands on a Hard Body (1997). Documentary by first-time director S. R. Bindler follows a slew of Longview residents as they vie to win a new truck by means of a last-man-standing marathon. Surprisingly engaging, it will have you cheering aloud for your favorite contestants.

The Zapruder film (1963). Arguably the most important film ever made in Texas was not a Hollywood production at all. On November 22, 1963, Abraham Zapruder, a clothing manufacturer, set out to record President John F. Kennedy's visit to Dallas with a home movie camera— and wound up capturing the assassination of the president on film, thus chronicling the turning point of a nation. The 35th anniversary of JFK's death marked the release of a hugely affecting documentary on Zapruder himself and the historically invaluable "Zapruder film."

Texas Music Is More Than Just a Two-Step

Since the turn of the twentieth century, Texans have made key contributions to many musical genres. Trying to list them all would send this chapter right off the scale, so we'll just hit a few high notes. Bob Wills, for example, grew up in Turkey and during the '30s and '40s headed the nation's most popular band, the Texas Playboys. Crowning achievements from the "King of Western Swing" include classics emeritus such as "San Antonio Rose" and "Faded Love." Regardless of which tunes you hear, however, it's certain that where there's Wills, there's a sway.

Another rhythmic royal was Scott Joplin of Texarkana, better known as the "King of Ragtime." He was a major innovator of the catchy, syncopated sound that greatly influenced jazz. Later, performers such as tenor saxmen Arnett Cobb, Ornette Coleman, and King Curtis and trumpeters Hot Lips Page, Milt Larkin, and Charlie Teagarden jazzed up Texas music, too.

A whole palette of blues singers also hailed from Texas, including Huddie Ledbetter, a.k.a. Leadbelly (the nickname derived from his strength and stamina—a distinct advantage in fistfights and in prison work gangs). Leadbelly was a convicted murderer, but he also killed 'em with his songs—he wrote "Goodnight, Irene" and "Rock Island Line," among many others—and his serenade to Governor Pat Neff resulted in a pardon.

Later, blues greats included Navasota's Mance Lipscomb, who preferred to style himself as a "songster" and who went undiscovered until age 65. Another famous Texas-born musician was gravel-voiced Janis Joplin, the Port Arthur native who was a relative rarity—a female, Anglo blues star—and who died in 1970 at age 27 of a heroin overdose.

Inevitably, Texans also scored big in rock and roll. In particular, a gawky, bespectacled Lubbock boy proved a true buddy to the genre; Buddy Holly's distinctively melodic, highly danceable tunes, like "That'll Be the Day" and "Peggy Sue," galvanized American pop music for two years before his death in a 1959 plane crash at age 22.

Nearly as influential was Roy Orbison of Wink, whose trademarks were his ubiquitous dark glasses and a soaring, operatic voice that powered hits like "Pretty Woman" and "Only the Lonely."

From the late '60s through the '70s, the Austin counter-culture that sprang up around the sprawling University of Texas campus spawned scores of musical groups, including "acid rockers" like the 13th Floor Elevators, headed by Roky Erickson.

And, of course, Texans always excelled at country and western music, too. Hall of Famer Ernest Tubb, born in Ellis County, electrified the genre—literally—by the mid-'40s, when he became the first performer to wire his guitar so that his band, the Texas Troubadours, could be heard above honky-tonk hullabaloo. George Jones of Sarasota is one of the greatest country singers of all time, recording hits like the transcendent "He Stopped Loving Her Today."

More recent practicioners of Texas country include Willie Nelson, Waylon Jennings, and Jerry Jeff Walker, whose self-styled "outlaw" movement produced a most distinctive Texan sound. Their influence inspired greats like Lyle Lovett and it still continues today. Combined with the '60s- and '70s-era rock scene in Austin, and the state's ethnic influences—German polka, Mexican *corridos* (ballads), and more—they made Texas music the diverse and accomplished entertainment it is today.

Following is another chronological list—again, by no means definitive—of ten great Texas albums that offer a sampling of Lone Star lyrics and regional riffs:

Willis Alan Ramsey, *Willis Alan Ramsey* (1972). This album, highlighted by the cuts "Ballad of Spider John" and "Northeast Texas Women," contains almost no throwaway tunes.

Doug Sahm, *Doug Sahm & the Band* (1973). After earlier indulging in a pseudo-Beatle approach to exploit the British-invasion craze, Sahm recorded this big-label (Atlantic) with guest appearances by the likes of Bob Dylan, Dr. John, and David "Fathead" Newman—as well as a Texas stalwart, accordionist Flaco Jimenez.

Jerry Jeff Walker, *Viva Terlingua!* (1973). A quintessentially Texan masterpiece by (gasp) a native of New Jersey, this venerable album earned Walker a massive following that, more than a quarter century later, still remains fiercely loyal. Walker provides definitive versions of Guy Clark's

"Desperados Waiting for a Train" and Gary P. Nunn's "London Homesick Blues."

Commander Cody & His Lost Planet Airmen, *Live From Deep in the Heart of Texas* (1974). This wacky, eclectic album showcases a variety of sounds, and the cover art and liner notes by artist Jim Franklin are equally appealing and true to the era.

Willie Nelson, *Red-Headed Stranger* (1975). A Texas cult hero during the '70s, Nelson was long merely a songwriter, achieving his own performing success only when he came home from Nashville. Good songs, amply dolloped with Texanness, include the stellar "Blue Eyes Cryin' in the Rain." Great guitar licks, too—plus that wonderful, one-of-a-kind Willified voice.

Delbert McClinton, *Keeper of the Flame* (1979). This Texas rhythm-and-blues blowout is a keeper, even though the snakebit label (Capricorn) wasn't; it joined the list of other record companies that folded, mysteriously, after producing McClinton releases. Great songs, skillful production, and a sexy guy.

Lyle Lovett, *Pontiac* (1987). Lovett is the most talented, original, and enjoyable Texas artist recording today; every single album of his is worth a listen. This one, his second, is my favorite, just because of the whimsical "If I Had a Boat" and the poignant "Walk Through the Bottomland."

His first self-titled album (1986) is equally wonderful, though, as are *Lyle Lovett and His Large Band* (1989) and *Joshua Judges Ruth* (1992). Try one; you'll Lovett.

Spinning Around the Sun, Jimmie Dale Gilmore (1993). Gilmore had plied his musical trade for decades before he hit it big. His twangy, clangy voice is an acquired taste, but it perfectly suits his Texas-drenched lyrics.

Nanci Griffith, *Other Voices, Other Rooms* (1993). Her early days as an Austin folksinger gave the girlish Griffith a deep appreciation for Texas songwriting. This album pays tribute to many of her favorite lyricists, Lone Star and otherwise, and includes gems such as "Tecumseh Valley," penned by the late great Townes Van Zandt.

Robert Earl Keen, *Gringo Honeymoon* (1994). Like Lyle Lovett (a former housemate during their A&M years), Keen has produced several equally fine albums. This one gets my nod for two ultra-Texan theme songs, "Barbeque" and "Merry Christmas From the Family." Many other original Keen tunes are now country-folk-rock staples, such as "The Road Goes on Forever" and "Sing One for Sister." All are keenly felt pleasures.

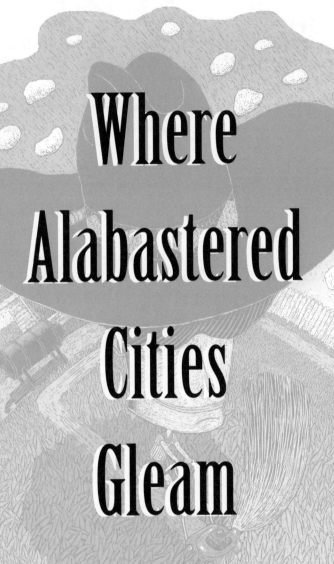

Where
Alabastered
Cities
Gleam

Some errors have become so engrained in the collective consciousness of the nation that most Americans don't even think of them as true or false. One such generalized falsehood is that Texas is an untamed wilderness. So pervasive (and persuasive) is the idea of Texas as a wild and woolly wasteland that many out-of-staters persist in viewing the state as a shoot-'em-up frontier. This is partly Texas' fault: We love our tall tales and we love our fame, however dubious.

Millennial Texas, though, is a thoroughly urban place. Three-fourths of the state's residents live in cities, and three of those cities are in the nation's top 10 for size. So, despite the hype and hoopla about cowboys and cattle and wide-open spaces, most of us Texans today are city slickers (goldarnit), and a review of our supposed rurality is in order. Read on for a lo-cal lesson in how (and where) Texans go to town.

DALLAS

No other city in Texas is as self-aware, as image-conscious, as Big D. This is because Dallas is a nonpareil combination of style, piety, and wealth. It is about saving face and being saved through faith, and about manners as much as manors. No matter what, Dallas holds its well-groomed head up. It survived the devastating blow of the Kennedy assassination and accepted with good grace the depiction of its residents as the cartoon characters of that inimitable television prime-time sudser of the same name.

In many ways, the city seems a contradiction in terms; for example, some of its most affluent districts are dry— meaning they do not permit the public sale of alcohol— because of the region's almost ubiquitous Bible-Belt beliefs. At the same time, the matrons there are indisputably elegant as befits women who live in the hometown of Neiman Marcus, the venerable purveyor of chic to the sleek.

Since its founding in 1907, Neiman Marcus has been a trailblazer for Texas fashion consciousness (some residents refer to it as "Needless Markup," for its goods are pricey as well as polished). Inevitably, the store's influence affected the entire city, which today boasts the internationally renowned Apparel Mart, a savvy and soignée center for design. In Dallas, stylishness is next to Godliness: both, according to some residents, are equally divine.

HOUSTON

If, as the saying goes, Dallas is the pretty sister with the ugly personality, then Houston is the ugly sister with charm. As big and brash as its namesake, Sam Houston, it is a city of limitless possibilities; it simply oozes ambition and energy. It also oozes, period; its coastal location, swampy soil, and relentless humidity have wilted many a tender transplant. (No wonder a common greeting is "How's bayou?") Houston is the nation's second largest port, and is also famed for its medical center, where doctors Michael DeBakey and Denton Cooley made their names as heart surgery pioneers.

The city, however, is probably best-known outside Texas as the site of Mission Control—as in "Houston, we have a problem." And Houston has had its problems: The city's rise as a space center paralleled its rapid population growth, and residents used to joke that the city had a space center but no space.

The city, though, truly rocketed to fame—not with NASA but with the oil and gas industry. Primarily and historically, Houston is an oil town, and its prosperity has always waxed and waned with the fortunes of the "bidness." The massive towers of Shell Oil, Tenneco, Pennzoil, and other giants have helped create the city's dramatic skyline.

Equally distinctive, in terms of architecture, is the Astrodome; as a then-unique center for baseball and other professional sports, it hit a dome run. (The fact that it was long ago outstripped by larger covered stadiums doesn't faze Houstonians; after all, their city built the first.) When it was built in 1965, Houston dubbed the Astrodome the Eighth Wonder of the World. Decades later, visitors may find it about an eighth as wonderful as it once was, but it still remains a testament to Houston's modern sensibilities and forward thinking. Houston is one kick-Astro kind of place.

SAN ANTONIO

The most romantic and colorful place in Texas, San Antonio is a big city with a small-town feel. Its single most salient feature is its Hispanic heritage; nowhere else north of the border can a visitor soak up so much laid-back, Mexican-style hospitality (and so much grease—the city teems with great little Tex-Mex joints, where, lard help us, grease is a primary ingredient).

Atmospheric adobe buildings and luxuriant flowering plants line its winding streets which, at least once, will take even seasoned visitors somewhere they didn't set out to go. Getting lost in San Antonio, a 300-year-old town, is part of the experience. An old joke has it that San Antonio was laid out by a drunk cowboy on a blind mule in a sandstorm.

San Antonio is also home to the state's number-one tourist attraction, the Alamo, which was once a mission, then a fort, and is now, quite literally, a shrine. The Alamo once witnessed a terrifying siege, but the only thing scary about it now are the volunteer "protectors" who patrol its interior walls. These Alamo defenders guard the building against noise, fractious toddlers, and visitors who unwittingly talk in above-normal conversational tones, as if the average daily crowd of 5,000 could be expected to file silently and reverently through. It's worth braving these lions, however, to marvel at the Alamo's size; despite looming large in American history, the building itself is surprisingly small. Its thick adobe walls, though, still provide welcome relief from San Antonio's fierce sun.

Tourists fighting meltdown from the heat also hie themselves to the tropically resplendent River Walk—a winding, subterranean path of restaurants and shops that parallels both sides of the San Antonio River, offering everything from piñatas to piña coladas to pin-ya-to-the-wall crowds. Visitors also like barging onto the riverboats that ply the waterway in a regular stream. No question about it: San Antonio's rio has brio.

AUSTIN

Austin is a capital place to live. The permanent site of state government since 1850, Austin also boasts the University of Texas and an ever-burgeoning high-tech industry (you might say computers have made an in-Dellible impression on the city). Lawmakers meet every other year in the handsomely renovated Capitol building, which was deliberately constructed to rise seven feet taller than its counterpart in Washington, D.C. It's considered good luck to stand on the rotunda floor's giant star and clap to hear the deafening echo (unless you're a legislator; then the deafening noise is that of Texans demanding your return to work).

From UT comes the city's strong academic bent—its residents are the most highly educated in the state—and a hippie-dippie influence; during the '60s the "Drag" (the portion of Guadalupe Street that skirts the western edge of the campus) was the Southwest's Haight-Ashbury, and it still provides the best people-watching in town. The university has also contributed to the local writing and moviemaking scenes, both of which earn straight A's for quality and diversity.

And though Austin's cyber-community presents an image of pale-skinned Gollumlike nerds glued to their computer screens, the city is equally forceful in environmental awareness and outdoor activities. Gorgeous parks and wilderness preserves abound in and around the city.

Austinites also know how to party, celebrating everything from Eeyore's birthday—an annual April celebration of silliness that is pooh-poohed by the humorless, to Spamarama—a music and pop culture bash dedicated to the much-maligned potted meatstuff (and at which attendees are likely to get potted, too). Austin's nonpareil spring and fall weather lures runners, walkers, cyclists, frisbee fanatics, kite flyers, and other fresh-air and exercise lovers by the thousands.

FORT WORTH

Although Fort Worth has long been saddled with the reputation of being countrified, this folksy city revels in its image as the most relentlessly western of Texas towns.

It's also known as Cowtown, and its stockyards—replete with cowboys and cattle (and serious stinkola)—look much as they did a hundred years ago. City fathers and mothers ride herd over trail drives through the city, and herds of visitors come to sample its rodeos, saloons, steak-houses, and hat-and-boot emporia.

The city's contrast with Dallas, its longtime rival, couldn't be more pronounced, and yet Fort Worth has corralled plenty of sophisticated sites, too. Two jewels, for example, are the Kimbell Art Museum and the Amon Carter Museum of Western Art—stellar collections by homegrown millionaire-philanthropists that help make Fort Worth a Texas star.

EL PASO

More than 400 years old and more than 500 miles from the state capital, this desert metropolis is technically Texan but, spiritually and culturally, it is a product of that amorphous but distinct region known as the border-lands. Its full name was originally "El Paso del Norte" (Spanish for "the pass of the north") because it lies in a natural plateau between two mountain ranges—the Franklins to the north and the Sierra de Juarez range just across the Rio Grande.

Explorers as far back as Cabeza de Vaca passed through the pass of the north, but today its geographical remote-ness from mainland Texas means that many Texans take a pass on visiting there, and most lawmakers rarely pass legislation to improve the city's fortunes. El Pasoans, however, have their compensations. Labor, for example, is cheap and plentiful; thousands of folks from its sister city, Juarez, cross the river daily to work north of *la frontera*—the sunny side, economically speaking. El Pasoans also enjoy the dry desert climate that is highly conducive to mental and physical health.

Most residents of this border city speak both Spanish and English; conversations commonly ping-pong back and forth between the two languages, to the dismay of monolingual visitors.

All in all, Texas cities reflect the wealth of diversity that the state itself is known for. No matter what type of culture or terrain you are looking for, chances are you can find it in the Lone Star State. And, once you find it, you may discover that you don't want to leave. That's the mystique of Texas.

Index

INDEX

Tequila, 84
"That'll Be The Day," 105
13th Floor Elevators, 105
Tigua Indians, 15
To Kill a Mockingbird, 101
Tony Lamas boots, 39
Torn, Rip, 100
Traffic, 8–10
Trip to Bountiful, The, 101
True Stories, 101
Tubb, Ernest, 105
Turkey, 104
Two Rode Together, 98, 99

U

University of Texas, 6, 21, 100, 101, 114, 115
Urban Cowboy, 100
Uvalde, 38, 101

V

Vaca, Cabeza de, 116
Van Zandt, Townes, 108
Viva Terlingua!, 107

W

Waco, 3, 13, 88
Walk on the Wild Side, 14

"Walk Through the Bottomland," 108
Walker, Jerry Jeff, 106, 107
Walker, Mary Willis, 93
Waltz Across Texas, 100
Wayne, John, 98, 99
Weather, 18
Webb, Walter Prescott, 92
Well-Spent Life, A, 98
West Texas, 3, 4, 14, 30, 88, 93
Wharton, 101
Widmark, Richard, 99
Willis, 82
Willis Alan Ramsey, 106
Wills, Bob, 104
Wind, The, 93
Wings, 98
Wink, 105
Wittliff, Bill, 95
Wolf and the Buffalo, The, 95
Woman of the People, A, 94
Written on the Wind, 98

Z

Zapruder, Abraham, 102
Zapruder film, the, 102
Zirl, Robert, 82

About the Author

Native Texan **Anne Dingus** graduated from Rice University and resides in Austin. A senior editor at *Texas Monthly* magazine, she is also the author of *The Truth About Texas* and *More Texas Sayings Than You Can Shake a Stick At*.